MURDER & MAYHEM
— IN —
EAST TENNESSEE

DEWAINE A. SPEAKS

THE
History
PRESS

Published by The History Press
Charleston, SC
www.historypress.com

Front cover, top left: *Knoxville News-Sentinel*; *top center*: Rebecca Henry; *top right*: *Knoxville News-Sentinel*; *bottom*: *Clarion-Ledger*.
Back cover: author's collection: *inset*: Federal Bureau of Investigation.

First published 2020

Manufactured in the United States

ISBN 9781467144704

Library of Congress Control Number: 2020940195

Notice: The information in this book is true and complete to the best of our knowledge. It is offered without guarantee on the part of the author or The History Press. The author and The History Press disclaim all liability in connection with the use of this book.

*This work is dedicated to our grandchildren, Allison, Laura, Rebecca and Aaron,
and to our great-grandchildren, Eliza and Elliot.
I hope they will always remember the good times we had, whether we were
playing games or going on "mystery trips."*

CONTENTS

FOREWORD

We may ask why people should be interested in reading about the murder and mayhem in the life story of others, but Dewaine Speaks has done an excellent job giving us the answer to that question with each story in *Murder and Mayhem in East Tennessee*. He arouses our curiosity with intimate details of families who suffer tragedy, and then he allows us to see glimpses of our own humanity as we search for answers as to why this may have happened and how we ourselves may have coped. We as readers need hope that we could survive in the midst of horror. We see survivors in Dewaine's book. We also see some successes, and most of all, we see caring communities surrounding those who are hurting because of tragedy.

I especially appreciate the empathetic manner with which Dewaine paints the tragic story of the death of my father, Captain Thomas Drinnen, MD, in World War II. *Mayhem* is defined as "violent or damaging disorder, chaos." War is mayhem. The world, East Tennessee and homes in Knoxville experienced the chaos and mayhem of the war. The story of Captain Drinnen is not a unique one from the early 1940s war era; perhaps you will find your own experiences somewhere in our family story. You may feel the same overwhelming sadness of family grief, the loneliness of the sudden loss of a parent or the triumph of survival as time and life march forward.

Dewaine Speaks knew the Drinnen boys when they were teenagers, growing up in the 1950s without a father. He knows we could be "rascals." He witnessed the quiet strength of our mother at all of our sporting events and her involvement in our lives. Yes, we had the "damaging disorder of mayhem" and all the scars attached to such loss, but we also had a loving, strong community of friends and family who supported our growth. Also, as Dewaine mentions, in 2010, we were fortunate to find a large bundle of letters from our dad that our mother had packed away and never touched again. Through these letters, we were allowed an insight into his personality and love for his family.

—Thomas B. Drinnen Jr., MD

"And Cain talked with Abel his brother: and it came to pass, when they were in the field, that Cain rose up against Abel his brother and slay him. And the Lord said unto Cain, where is Abel thy brother? And he said, I know not: am I my brother's keeper? And he said what hast thou done? The voice of thy brother's blood crieth unto me from the ground" (Genesis 4:8–10).

From the beginning of recorded history, as Cain killed Abel, brother has injured and killed brother, neighbor has injured and killed neighbor and stranger has injured and killed stranger. The motive behind each of these ungodly acts is as varied as the personalities of the parties involved; that is to say, the motives historically have been greed, jealousy, hatred and all other kinds of evil and misguided reasons.

Dewaine Speaks has selected for his book several of many notorious murder crimes perpetrated in East Tennessee. As a lawyer and a judge with over forty-two years of experience, much of it involving criminal law, I can state with certainty that Mr. Speaks has re-created each of these stories with the distilled and concentrated essence as to each crime that was committed.

I have some degree of familiarity with the Richards crime, perpetrated in my hometown of Oliver Springs, Tennessee, in 1940. As a young man, I knew Mayme Seinknecht when she was a local insurance agent. I also knew Tommy Diggs, the grade-school student who attempted to convey messages from the schoolteacher Richards to her sisters, who were ultimately found dead, and William F. Sharp, the funeral-home operator in Oliver Springs who conducted the funeral of the Richards sisters. I also knew Leonard Hacker, who worked for William Booth and conducted the funeral of Powder Brown. I have also discussed the Richards' murder with Mr. Diggs and the children of Sharp and Hacker.

Mr. Speaks has captured the essence of the Richards' murder mystery. I have no doubt that he has also captured the essence of the other murderous activities that are covered in his book *Murder and Mayhem in East Tennessee*.

As you read these stories of criminal activity so artfully crafted by Speaks, reflect on how much better the world would be if each individual had honored and followed the simple commandment "Thou shalt not kill" (Exodus 20:13).

I hope you enjoy reading Mr. Speaks's book as much as I did, and I highly recommend it to you.

—Joe Van Hook, attorney-at-law

ACKNOWLEDGEMENTS

The assistance received from the following individuals and organizations is greatly appreciated:

Jack E. Webb, Ruth Ellen Baldwin, Rebecca Bottoms, Jim Hackworth, Daniel and Carolyn Harrison, Howard M. Samples, Jerry and Vicki Kerr, Charles and Judy Rainwater, McClung Collection, Rebecca Henry, Charles Plummer, Carly R. Kennedy, Federal Bureau of Investigation, Tennessee State Library and Archives, Joe Van Hook, Deloris Steel, Aaron Speaks, Mary Hammond, Powell Community Library, Allison and Andrew Whitener, Becky Walden, Library of Congress, Tracy and Eddie Speeks, Laura and Kevin Davis, Dr. Tom and Anita Hunter Drinnen, Cindy Webb, Terri Webb, East Tennessee Historical Society, Cherel Henderson, Charlie and Clara Murphy, Carlene and Tom Clevenger, Suzanne and James Henry, David and Michelle Speaks, Mildred Myers, Dana and Wayne Howard, Lester and Theresa Speeks, Winnie and Don Utterback, Hiwassee River Heritage Center, Darlene Goins, Dr. William and Marjorie Waldrop, Haskel "Hack" Ayers, Debra Nelson, Codi Provins, Charlie Davis, Robbie Underwood, Oliver Springs Historical Society, Hampton Inn (Caryville, Tennessee) and Hack Ayers Auctioneer and Real Estate Company.

INTRODUCTION

Although there are many incidents of murder and mayhem from which to choose, an attempt has been made to research and write about those with interesting subplots or those that have some historical significance. With the information given about some of the unsolved murders, readers might draw their own conclusions regarding guilty parties. It is not, however, the writer's intent to try to do what the law enforcement officials were often unable to do.

Family members and friends of the murder victims were often frustrated with the police as the investigations proceeded. Much of this frustration came because the investigators were often not quite able to obtain sufficient evidence with which to charge a suspect. The families wanted justice, and they wanted it immediately.

The book covers approximately the same number of mayhem events as murder cases. Some of the murder cases were solved; some were not. Each chapter covers stories that shocked communities, affected lives and often created mayhem. In some chapters, mayhem, murder and unexpected death are all present.

James Earl Ray, who had already killed Dr. Martin Luther King, created mayhem in the whole country and especially in East Tennessee when he was sent to Brushy Mountain State Penitentiary. Incredibly, he led six other men in a short-lived escape. He actually got married while incarcerated at the penitentiary.

Several thousand Cherokee Indians from East Tennessee were force-marched on what would later be called the "Trail of Tears." An unknown number perished.

In the "Hankins Murder" case and in the triple killings in Oliver Springs, chaos and confusion resulted from the wrongful arrest of and public accusations toward innocent people.

East Tennesseans, the United States Army and a village in England were caught up in mayhem during the war year of 1943. Dr. Thomas Drinnen, a popular physician in Knoxville, left his wife and three small boys and sailed for England in preparation for treating wounded soldiers on the battlefield. The shock felt in a British village and in East Tennessee when he accidentally died of carbon monoxide poisoning was evident in the contemporary newspaper articles that appeared in both countries.

Even though Clarence Leon Raby made the FBI's Ten Most Wanted list, it became obvious that he would kill only when someone pulled a gun on him.

Jake and C.H. Butcher brought about mayhem with their banking scandal that at the time was unsurpassed in scope in the nation's history. Jake was the principal promoter of the 1982 World's Fair in Knoxville, Tennessee. By all accounts, the six-month affair was a success. Days after the close of the fair, the Butcher banks started crumbling. Thousands of investors lost their life savings. The Butchers lost their freedom.

1

JAMES EARL RAY GOES TO "THE END OF THE LINE"

The nickname "The End of the Line" was a good description of the maximum-security prison that for hundreds of felons was just that. It was definitely not a place for the faint-of-heart, for either prisoners or the guards who worked there. An old saying has reappeared as the caption on modern-day T-shirts: "Brushy was the damnation of many an evil man and the salvation of a humble few."

Brushy Mountain State Penitentiary was built snug up against the Cumberland Mountains in Petros, Tennessee, in 1896. The original wood structure was replaced in the 1920s with a masonry edifice that somewhat resembled a castle.

The main reason for the prison's location near the mountains was the vast stores of coal inside the mountains. Most of the prisoners were assigned the duty of digging coal, and they were assigned tonnage quotas. Well into the twentieth century, for those who failed to meet their quotas, a merciless beating with a leather strap awaited them.

There were very few attempts to escape, and almost none that were successful. Escape attempts were significantly discouraged by the howling bloodhounds kept in a compound just outside the prison walls.

In 1977, James Earl Ray, the man convicted of killing Martin Luther King, entered the confines of Brushy Mountain's gruesome and brutal world. He had previously been incarcerated in two other maximum-security prisons: four years in Leavenworth, Kansas, for theft and twenty-five years in the Missouri State Penitentiary in Jefferson City, Missouri, for cashing fraudulent money orders.

Weapon that killed Martin Luther King. Clarion-Ledger.

With eighteen years left on his sentence, he had escaped from the Missouri penitentiary by concealing himself in the bottom of a container filled with loaves of bread. He immediately fled to Mexico, where he stayed for several months. He was officially on escapee status from the Jefferson City prison when he shot King in Memphis on April 4, 1968.

At Brushy Mountain, Ray was to quickly learn that his new home was just as violent as the one from which he had escaped. Ray would occupy cell no. 28, and he was assigned to work in the prison laundry. His prisoner identification number was 65477. Ray's job assignment immediately brought about outcries from the public, as some thought this job was too cushy for a man who had been convicted of cold-blooded murder. This, however, would be his work assignment as long as he was in "Brushy."

After King's murder and several days of investigative work by the police, it was determined that Ray had used the name John Willard at the boardinghouse in Memphis from which he fired the fatal shot. In his haste leaving the scene, he either discarded or accidentally dropped the 30.06 hunting rifle he used to murder Dr. King. When Ray's fingerprints were found on the weapon, he became the subject of the largest manhunt in U.S. history. He was immediately placed on the FBI's Ten Most Wanted list. His flight would last sixty-five days and lead law enforcement agents to Canada, England, Portugal and then back to England. At various times,

Left: FBI's Most Wanted flyer pertaining to James Earl Ray. *Federal Bureau of Investigation.*

Below: FBI's canceled flyer after the capture of James Earl Ray. *Federal Bureau of Investigation.*

he used the aliases Eric Starvo Galt, John Willard, Harvey Lowmeyer, Paul Bridgman and Ramon George Sneyd.

The following teletype directive from FBI Director J. Edgar Hoover, which went to the three thousand agents working on the case, shows the amount of pressure government officials were under as they were pressed to find the killer.

We are continuing with all possible diligence and dispatch....The investigation is nationwide in scope as countless suspects are being processed and physical evidence is being traced. You may be completely assured that this investigation will continue on an expedited basis until the matter has been resolved. Leads are to be afforded immediate, thorough, imaginative attention. You must exhaust all possibilities from such leads as any one lead could result in the solution of this most important investigation. SAC [Special Agent in Charge] will be held personally responsible for any failure to promptly and thoroughly handle investigations in this matter.

Feeling the same pressure, early in the manhunt, U.S. Attorney General Ramsey Clark established a situation room with cots on the fifth floor of the U.S. Justice Department building. Food was brought in for the people working twenty-four hours every day on the legal components of the case. Clark would later make the following statement regarding that time: "It was a huge operation. I didn't go home. I just stayed there all the time. I had a little place in my office where I'd sleep. It was the biggest investigation ever conducted, for a single crime, in U.S. history."

Fingerprints and other leads turned up by the FBI in Los Angeles, Birmingham, Atlanta and Toronto conclusively identified James Earl Ray as the killer of Martin Luther King. On June 8, 1968, Ray was arrested at London's Heathrow Airport as he was trying to board a plane for Brussels, Belgium.

Even though he knew he had been caught, he remained defiant and told the British police officers: "Look! They got me mixed up with some guy called James Earl Ray. My name is Ramon George Sneyd. I never met this Ray guy in my life. I don't know anything about this. They're just trying to pin something on me I didn't do."

After several days of extradition hearings, on July 18, 1968, an Air Force C-135, with Ray on board, took off a few minutes before midnight from the American air base in Lakenheath, Suffolk. After flying all night on a secret mission, the plane landed in Memphis at 3:48 a.m. on July 19. Shelby County Sheriff William Morris assumed responsibility for the prisoner. Ray was whisked off to a special secure cell that had cost Shelby County over $100,000 to construct.

After Ray was convicted of killing King and sentenced to ninety-nine years of incarceration, he was sent to a state prison in Nashville. In May 1971, he was transferred to Brushy Mountain State Penitentiary in East

Above: Brushy Mountain State Penitentiary. *Author's collection.*

Left: Rock wall, guardhouse and barbed wire at Brushy Mountain Penitentiary. *Author's collection.*

Ray's prison cell no. 28. *Author's collection.*

Tennessee. He almost immediately tried to escape by crawling through an air duct but was blocked by a high-temperature steam line.

After six years, James Earl Ray had somewhat faded from the memories of much of the population. The prison guards and his fellow prisoners knew of his reputation but started viewing him as just another prisoner. Some of them later said that they should have known that Ray was likely to be plotting a way out. No one thought that escape was possible, even though Ray had made the following, almost prophetic statement to the news media: "They wouldn't have me in a maximum security prison if I wasn't interested in getting out….You always have it in the back of your mind. When you come to the penitentiary, you checkout various escape routes. You file them away, and if the opportunity arises, well you can go ahead. I suspect that everyone in here has it in the back of his mind. The only thing is whether they have the fortitude to go through with it."

The rock walls were thirteen feet high and had a 2,300-volt electric strand of wire with razor-sharp edges running along the top. Scaling the walls would mean certain death. Experts were on record as saying, "Brushy is escape-proof."

On June 10, 1977, just before dark, dozens of prisoners in the large recreation yard started fighting and screaming. One inmate rolled around on the ground, claiming his leg had been broken. Guards, not immediately realizing that it was a well-planned ruse, entered the yard in an attempt to stop the melee.

This diversion was part of Ray's conceived, planned and carried-out escape scheme. Ray and six other prisoners had carried under their clothing several lengths of one-half-inch water pipe that, when quickly screwed together, formed a crude nine-foot ladder complete with a bent hook on top to secure it to the wall. Ray was the first to reach the top of the wall and slither under the wire. Six others followed. When Ray dropped to the ground, one of America's most notorious killers had escaped. The incredible had just happened. How could it be?

At the time of the escape, electricity and telephone service went dead inside the prison, raising suspicion that one or more prison employees had been part of a large, orchestrated conspiracy. This could be investigated later; for now, a manhunt had to be launched.

The last man clambering over the wall, Jerry Ward, convicted of bank robbery, was spotted by the guards and was hit in the arm and side of his face by blasts from a shotgun. The wounded man was quickly apprehended. The guards were surprised when he, almost gleefully, shouted, "Ray's out. James Earl Ray got away!"

Ray was out of prison, but he faced the steep Cumberland Mountains and its copperheads and rattlesnakes. Within an hour, 150 men with shotguns and miner's headlamps, along with bloodhounds, were on the trail of the escapees. As soon as telephone service was restored at the prison, the FBI in Washington, D.C., and Governor Ray Blanton in Nashville were contacted. James Earl Ray then had the distinction of being placed on the FBI's Ten Most Wanted list for the second time. The bureau printed forty thousand flyers bearing Ray's picture and circulated them across the nation. Dozens of agents were dispatched to Petros, Tennessee.

Governor Blanton activated members of the National Guard, and the day after the escape, six helicopters flew over the area with infrared heat-seeking scopes. Two more escapees were brought in that day, but Ray was still loose.

Coincidentally, at the time of Ray's escape, Martin Luther King's father, "Daddy" King, was scheduled to preach at a Baptist church forty miles away in Knoxville. Some law-enforcement officers feared that a conspiracy was underway and that the elder King's life was in danger. Knoxville media reporters asked King if he had any comment about the manhunt that was

Part of wall that Ray and six others scaled. *Author's collection.*

underway for the man convicted of killing his son. He told them, "I hope they don't kill him. Let's hope he doesn't get killed. You're looking at the face of a black man who hates nobody." With Ray and others still at large, King said that he had a bodyguard at all times and that he had "stopped checking into hotels in my own name a long time ago."

Governor Blanton gave the nation assurance and apprehension at the same time when he said that the National Guardsmen and members of law enforcement would not shoot Ray. He said they were under orders to use all possible restraint. Then he said, "The breakout was concocted, designed, and planned in such a manner that he could be in Guatemala now."

By Sunday, June 12, 1977, searchers with helicopters equipped with heat-seeking technology, National Guardsmen with night-vision glasses, the FBI with its surveillance cameras and hundreds of well-trained agents were exhausted and becoming frustrated. At this point, it was decided that it was time to quit relying on so much technology and go back to a time-proven method. It was time to call in the dogs.

Just before dark on Sunday night, the search for James Earl Ray was turned over to Sammy Joe Chapman and his two female bloodhounds, Sandy and

Little Red. Interestingly, Chapman had trained these dogs to not bark, to stay perfectly silent as they sniffed along the trail of their prey.

Late in the night, and about eight miles north of the prison, the dogs picked up a "hot" scent, but even in their obvious excitement they stayed perfectly quiet. While the dogs were attempting to pull Chapman up the mountain, he radioed a brief message to searchers back at the prison: "We are on a hot trail!"

After about an hour, the dogs and their handler could hear someone running ahead of them. At about 2:00 a.m., they stopped briefly and heard nothing. The dogs kept pressing forward until they suddenly stopped and stood still except for the wagging of their tails. Chapman drew his .38 Smith & Wesson pistol and said to the pile of leaves, "Don't move or I'll shoot."

Martin Luther King's killer, scratched all over and weak from hunger, gave up without even a cross word. He was handcuffed and taken back to Brushy Mountain. Because of his haggard appearance, Ray was made to get out of a vehicle in front of the prison and walk through the entrance so that as many prisoners as possible could see him in his sorry state.

Chapman said of Ray, "For a 49-year-old man who didn't know the mountains, he didn't do bad." Ray told the ever-present reporters: "It's disappointing being caught. I wasn't happy being run down. I'd rather be out there, but it's not the end of the world. There's tomorrow."

On Friday, October 13, 1978, Ray again shocked the nation. He got married. Wearing a borrowed sports coat, he and Anna Sandhu, an employee of a Knoxville television station, repeated their vows inside the prison. Anna Sandhu Ray spent her wedding night with friends at a Knoxville restaurant. Ray spent his in his cell.

The bride, who met Ray while she was making preparations for her television station to interview the prisoner, said, "he has the most direct gaze of any man I've ever known. I've seen men look at me and turn their eyes away, but James will look right into your eyes and won't flinch. 'Do you like Picasso?' was the first thing he said to me." A few days later, she wrote to Ray and told him that she knew that he didn't have any visitors, but she would like to talk with him. She promised that she would not tell anything that he might tell her. He quickly wrote back that he would be happy for her to visit him.

Anna told friends that she was so nervous that she tripped as she entered the visitation room. She said that the waiting Ray smiled and said, "You probably believe all those things you've read about me, and if you do you're

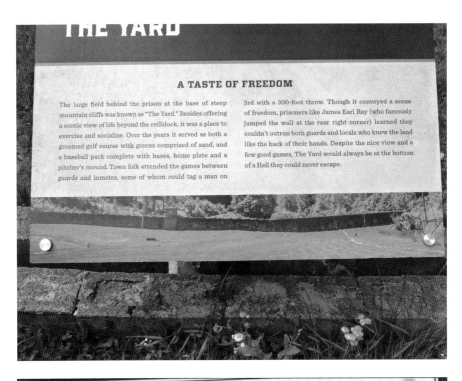

THE YARD

A TASTE OF FREEDOM

The large field behind the prison at the base of steep mountain cliffs was known as "The Yard." Besides offering a scenic view of life beyond the cellblock, it was a place to exercise and socialize. Over the years it served as both a groomed golf course with greens comprised of sand, and a baseball park complete with bases, home plate and a pitcher's mound. Town folk attended the games between guards and inmates, some of whom could tag a man on 3rd with a 300-foot throw. Though it conveyed a sense of freedom, prisoners like James Earl Ray (who famously jumped the wall at the rear right corner) learned they couldn't outrun both guards and locals who knew the land like the back of their hands. Despite the nice view and a few good games, The Yard would always be at the bottom of a Hell they could never escape.

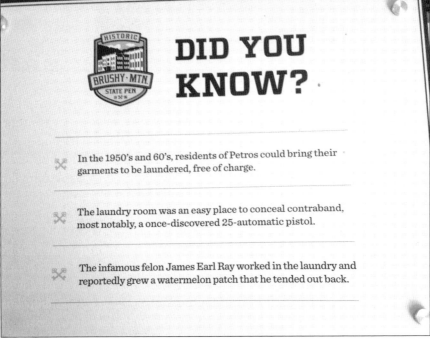

DID YOU KNOW?

HISTORIC BRUSHY · MTN. STATE PEN

In the 1950's and 60's, residents of Petros could bring their garments to be laundered, free of charge.

The laundry room was an easy place to conceal contraband, most notably, a once-discovered 25-automatic pistol.

The infamous felon James Earl Ray worked in the laundry and reportedly grew a watermelon patch that he tended out back.

FBI'S MOST WANTED

JAMES EARL RAY

Arguably its most infamous inmate, Martin Luther King, Jr.'s convicted assassin James Earl Ray spent years locked up in Brushy, notably spending time inside cell #28. After initially pleading guilty to the MLK Jr. shooting, he later recanted, claiming to be the patsy of a government conspiracy. Despite several escape attempts – one of which led to a massive FBI hunt in 1977, earning him dreaded D-Block isolation and years added to his sentence – he was reportedly an otherwise model prisoner. Once stabbed 22 times by four black inmates, he managed to survive. While suffering from liver disease in a Nashville correctional hospital, Ray promised Dr. King's son he was innocent shortly before he died in April of 1998. No evidence ever emerged to prove his claim.

Killer Captured
James Earl Ray, the convicted killer of civil rights leader Martin Luther King Jr., is escorted back into the Brushy Mountain State Prison by Warden Stonney Laine (left) and Deputy Warden Herman Davis after his capture early this morning. (UPI)

Opposite, top: Sign inside Brushy Mountain Penitentiary Museum. *Author's collection.*

Opposite, bottom: Informative sign inside Brushy Mountain Penitentiary Museum. *Author's collection.*

Above: Sign showing the capture of James Earl Ray. *Author's collection.*

convinced that I'm going to jump across this table." She said that Ray was a romantic man who wrote beautiful love letters.

After a few visits, she told Ray, "I love you." She said that he replied, "I'm glad." Shortly, Anna asked Ray if he would consider getting married. She said that, at first, he turned her down, but she ultimately changed his mind. She always said she believed in Ray's innocence until, one day, they were discussing King's murder, and Ray said, "Yeah, I killed him, so what if I did?" Anna said that this convinced her of Ray's guilt. She started divorce proceedings. After fourteen years of marriage, she was granted a divorce. More or less stating the obvious, Judge Jim Everett said, "This marriage was doomed from the beginning."

For the twenty-two years following his capture, James Earl Ray lived in cell number 28 and continued working in the laundry. He tried no more escapes and died on April 23, 1998, as the result of contracting hepatitis C. He had finally escaped.

After more than one hundred years of operation, in 2009, "The End of the Line" prison closed. The entire site is now operated as a museum and has become a popular destination—especially with civic organizations, church groups and classes of schoolchildren. Most visitors make certain that they locate cell 28, and nearly all describe their visit to the museum as being interesting yet sobering.

2

THE BOTCHED INVESTIGATION INTO THE MURDER OF MARY HANKINS

Fred Hankins drove his car for routine maintenance to Hensley Motor Service on Broadway in Fountain City, Tennessee. Don Severance, a high school student and part-time employee, drove Fred home in Fred's car and returned to the service center. When the work was completed, Severance returned to the Hankins home to pick up Hankins, and they returned to the service station. Fred then drove to visit his father, who lived nearby.

At about 5:00 p.m., Fred Hankins returned home expecting dinner to be ready. Instead, he discovered his wife, Mary, lying in a pool of blood. His first reaction was to run to his next-door neighbor, C.L. Holt, for help. Holt quickly called for an ambulance while Mrs. Holt rushed into the Hankins home. She screamed when she saw the awful scene.

An ambulance took Mary to St. Mary's Hospital, about five miles away, where she died within thirty minutes. The doctors removed a .32-caliber slug from her brain.

The date was Saturday, March 31, 1951. The Hankins home was located in the Harrill Hills section of Fountain City. Nothing like this had ever happened in the comfortable neighborhood. As news spread of the murder, dozens of neighbors quickly converged on the home, contaminating the crime scene to the extent that the murderer might never be identified. Investigators used this somewhat dubious excuse for not having attempted to lift fingerprints from the inside and outside of the front door and the doorbell.

The home of Mary Hankins. *Howard Samples.*

It was known that the killer used the front door to gain entry, because a neighbor across the street saw the killer come and go. While working in her yard, Mary Elizabeth Schumaker saw a man driving a black 1950 Ford park on the street in front of the Hankins home. The man, she said, "Was tall, lanky, and slightly stooped and was wearing a powder blue summer suit and a brown hat." She said that the man looked at the Hankinses' mailbox before he walked up to the door and knocked. She remembered that the man stayed in the house about twenty minutes and then walked briskly to his car and sped away.

She said that she thought the summer suit did not seem to be heavy enough because of the coolness of the day. She indicated that she herself was wearing three sweaters at the time. Schumaker did not mention that the man was wearing gloves, which makes the decision not to try lifting fingerprints even more puzzling. From Schumaker's observations, the man had almost certainly touched the doorknob on the inside and outside.

Schumaker said she saw the man ring the Hankinses' doorbell several times until Mary came to the door. After a brief conversation, the man entered the house. Schumaker told the police, "You couldn't have counted to

The home of Mr. and Mrs. C.L. Holt. *Author's collection.*

12 before the man entered the house after knocking." Investigators believed he likely had a gun aimed at Mary Hankins, because the people who knew her felt sure she would not willingly let a stranger into her house.

The Knox County Coroner believed that Mary Hankins was shot while lying down. He theorized that the victim was attempting to escape when she was knocked to the floor and shot. A dishcloth on the family's sofa led him to believe that a brief conversation had taken place between the two.

Sheriff Clarence Walter "Buddy" Jones took on the lead role in the investigation. Jones and Chief Deputy Paul H. Lilly said from the start that they had no credible leads. Nothing was missing from the house, and nothing was out of place. Jones stated, "There are no motives. It's a most baffling murder." In spite of having nothing to go on, Sheriff Jones went out on a limb when he said that he "would not sleep until the murder was solved."

Two days after the murder, and with a full-fledged investigation getting underway, a funeral service was conducted for Mary Tabler Hankins at Corryton's Graveston Baptist Church, the church she had attended since she was a child. She was buried in the church cemetery. Hundreds of Mary's friends, neighbors and those she had worked with at Standard Knitting Mills

Mary Elizabeth Schumacher's home. *Author's collection.*

attended the funeral. Many from this group would call the sheriff's office every day for months to see if any progress was being made in solving the case. It was obvious that everyone was impatient for the perpetrator to be brought to justice.

Sheriff Jones put up $100 of his own money as a reward for information that would lead to the arrest and conviction of the perpetrator. Businessman Tom Dempster, Knoxville City Councilman Cas Walker and others quickly pledged enough to raise the reward to $2,000. The amount eventually reached $20,000.

Three days after the murder, Fred Hankins belatedly discovered that Mary's watch was missing and believed that it was likely taken during the murder. He reported to the police that something had been taken from his house, after all. Incredibly, instead of immediately sending a description to area pawnshops, the police waited five months before contacting pawnshops with a description of the watch and a message to contact the police if it was pawned. The police circular, by now worthless, read as follows: "Attention pawn shops and police burglary detachments. Look out for a lady's yellow gold wrist watch, Gruen make, Model 21; movement,

Church where Mary Hankins's funeral was conducted. *Author's collection.*

Mary Hankins's tombstone with her picture. *Author's collection.*

2-753785; Case No. 5922-363. Jewelry repair identifications on inside bottom of case: J-G-4-9-4."

Seasoned detectives shook their heads when they learned of the lengthy delay in getting the watch's description out to the public. This came on top of the controversial decision not to lift fingerprints from the Hankins house because so many neighbors had crowded in. The same experienced lawmen thought that since the killer was known to have touched the front doorknob, there was a possibility that at least one print could have been lifted.

In the days following the murder, Sheriff Jones was almost desperate to locate a suspect. The first suspect was picked up for questioning simply because someone spotted him wearing a light blue suit and a brown hat. His name was never released, and he was promptly released.

On two different occasions, Mary Hankins's cousin Bill Tabler was questioned. Sheriff Jones had learned from family members that Tabler became upset when he unsuccessfully tried to borrow money from her. After the lengthy interviews, Jones released Tabler, saying, "I have questioned this man for two days, and I have nothing on him up to now."

To add to the confusion, a bizarre incident occurred. A close neighbor of the Hankinses was severely beaten in her own basement by a man wearing a mask. He admonished her to "keep your mouth shut." It seemed obvious that this incident was connected to the murder of Mary Hankins, but the reason for her beating was never determined. It was clear, however, that someone thought she had seen something or knew something that she should not tell.

On June 17, a farmer named John Johnson and his son went to their favorite place to wash their car, beside a creek that runs along Norris Freeway (U.S. 441), about eight miles from the murder site. It was a popular location for washing cars. While there, Johnson went to get a bucket of water and saw the glint of a pearl-handled pistol. The .32-caliber Colt was lying in only six inches of water when Johnson picked it up.

Johnson noticed that only one cartridge had been fired and the remaining five cartridges were still in the gun. The Johnsons took the weapon to Sheriff Jones, who instantly realized that they had found the murder weapon. To prevent this information from reaching the killer, he asked the Johnsons to keep their findings secret for three weeks.

Sheriff Jones booked a flight to Washington, D.C., and went directly to the FBI's ballistic laboratory. To the surprise of the sheriff and the laboratory personnel, good fingerprints were lifted from the five bullets still in the gun. They further determined that the fingerprints had been on the weapon when it was thrown in the water. R.S. Allen wrote that one of

Site along Norris Freeway where the Hankins murder weapon was found. *Author's collection.*

the FBI employees said, "It is one of the most extraordinary findings that we have ever come across."

Five months after the murder, a private investigator who called himself Colonel Mayer came from Gulfport, Mississippi, to try to solve the case. Sheriff Jones said, "I've learned that a special investigator has been hired privately to solve the Hankins case....I don't care how the case is solved, so long as it is solved." Colonel Mayer, however, soon hit the same wall that the police had run into and left town without developing a single lead.

Clarence "Buddy" Jones had just a little over one year of law enforcement experience as sheriff when the Hankins murder case became his responsibility. His prior experience in law enforcement was his one-year stint as warden of Brushy Mountain State Penitentiary in Petros, Tennessee. Perhaps this inexperience led him to make the ill-advised and brash declaration that he would not sleep until the Hankins murder was solved. When several months had gone by and the case had not been solved, the sheriff acquired the nickname "Sleepless Buddy Jones." This cutting nickname contributed to the losing of his reelection bid to Austin Cate.

Because the murder had occurred in Knox County, newly elected Sheriff Cate had primary jurisdiction for the case, but Knoxville Police Chief Joe Kimsey was conducting a parallel investigation. Operating almost as rivals, they shared very little information with each other. Jealousy and friction between the two organizations almost certainly had an adverse effect on the investigation. While each received a tip from the same person, it was Kimsey who acted on it first. On February 10, 1953, he swore out an arrest warrant for Joseph Buick Hegler.

The tipster, an associate of Jessie Waldroup, indicated that Waldroup might have some information about the Hankins case. When interviewed by the police, Waldroup accused Hegler of murdering Mary Hankins. She said that she and Hegler had lived together in Detroit and Knoxville and that Hegler was the father of her youngest child. She stated that she was with Hegler when he went to the Hankins house while he was making his rounds selling magazines. He went into the house while she waited in the car. She said that when he hurriedly came back to the car, she asked him what had happened. She said that he told her, "I just had to kill a woman. I'll blow your head off if you don't keep your mouth shut." When the investigators pointed out to her that the witness from across the street had not mentioned a second person in the car, she replied that she had been slumped down in the front seat reading a newspaper.

Chief Kimsey contacted police in Aiken, South Carolina, where Hegler was employed, and they immediately arrested him. Kimsey flew to South Carolina in a chartered plane and returned with Hegler, who was then placed in Knoxville's city jail. Hegler insisted all along that on the day of the murder he was working in the Pisgah National Forest in North Carolina. He also said that he had never sold magazines in his life.

After Hegler had been in the Knoxville jail for a week, a speedy trial was held, because defense attorney Ray Jenkins had filed a habeas corpus writ seeking Hegler's release. During the trial, Criminal Court Judge J. Fred Bibb was shown the payroll records from Hegler's employer, E.I. Dupont Company, showing that he had definitely been in North Carolina on the day of the murder. Hegler was ordered released immediately. Attorney General Hal Clements said, "Hegler's alibi was better than if had been in jail." Authorities believed that the reason for this entire bizarre episode was due to a woman who felt she had been scorned. The competition between the Knoxville City Police Department and the Knox County Sheriff's Department, each racing to be the first to solve the case, likely caused this innocent man to be jailed.

The interrogation of Jessie Waldroup. Knoxville News-Sentinel.

Weeks and months passed without any promising leads or suspects turning up. Then, in November 1954, R.S. Allen wrote in his book *Murder in Harrill Hills* that a Knoxville bootlegger named Floyd Bruce furnished the authorities with information that implicated James William "Bill" Luallen in the Hankins murder.

Bruce stated that at about 5:00 p.m. on the day of the murder, he had delivered eighteen pints of whiskey to Buford Roberts's house on Rudy Street, about five miles north of downtown Knoxville. He said that, just as he arrived, a man named Bill Luallen came walking around Robert's house wearing a light blue shirt and light-colored pants. He was sure that the shirt and pants were splattered with blood.

Bruce said that in a conversation about a week after the murder, Roberts told him that the family had raised money to help Luallen get out of town. At that time, he quoted Roberts as saying, "He killed that Hankins woman as sure as anything."

Authorities knew that Luallen had been arrested in Iowa when he was in possession of a dark blue 1950 Ford. He was sent to prison in Atlanta and later transferred to Brushy Mountain State Prison in Petros. It was from there that he was brought to Knoxville for questioning.

Luallen admitted that he had been driving a blue 1950 Ford and that he had stolen a .32-caliber pistol. This was about all he would tell the authorities during two days of questioning. Because their evidence was largely circumstantial, he was returned to Brushy Mountain State Prison without being charged.

As the investigators dug deeper into the life of Bill Luallen, they learned that he had been a petty thief all of his adult life. His first conviction had been in 1939 for breaking into houses, and he was sentenced to six years in jail. In 1942, he was again convicted of housebreaking and served three years in jail. During the trial, he admitted that, until that time, he had broken into thirty-two homes. His record showed that he mostly stole guns and watches.

At the time Mary Hankins was murdered, Luallen was an escapee and was being hunted. The two Knox County investigators who had spent the most time on the case, Pat Patterson and John Beeler, always believed that Hankins was killed as the result of a bungled burglary.

As years went by, the newspapers stopped writing about the murder and the investigation. Gradually, people stopped talking about it. Obviously, investigators thought they knew the identity of the guilty person or persons. Those who followed the story closely always believed that the ineptness of the investigators allowed the brutal murder of a good and decent woman to forever go unsolved.

3
THE AMBUSH OF A UNIVERSITY DEAN

At 6:45 a.m. on the cold morning of February 8, 1990, Dr. Hyram Kitchen was on his way to work at the University of Tennessee in Knoxville. He drove to the end of his driveway and stopped to open a gate in the fence that surrounded his property. Dr. Kitchen raised horses on his small six-acre farm on Northboro Road in the Powell community in northern Knox County, Tennessee. As he approached the gate, a person stepped out from behind a clump of bushes and started firing a .22-caliber pistol at the professor. One bullet went through a hand, five plowed into his body and two entered the back of his head. His body was found one hundred feet from his car, its engine still running.

The Kitchen property was a small, six-acre farm located amid a multifamily subdivision in north Knox County. Nearby neighbors said they heard people arguing and then gunfire. One neighbor reported seeing someone running through the field behind the Kitchen home. Yvonne Kitchen, Dr. Kitchen's wife, told investigators that she heard the gunfire and was afraid to go outside. Robbery was quickly ruled out, because nothing was taken from the house.

Dr. Kitchen, fifty-seven, was only the second Dean of the College of Veterinarian Medicine at the University of Tennessee. For several years, he had been in the forefront of medical research that involved experiments using animals. Because of this, he and deans at other research schools had been receiving death threats for some time.

The home of Dr. Hyram Kitchen. *Author's collection.*

Kitchen's colleagues immediately told the police about the threats Kitchen had been receiving from a militant animal-rights extremist group. Several of the colleagues believed it was likely that this group had committed the murder, since that is what they had been threatening. Investigators learned that the animal-rights group had threatened to kill veterinary college deans at the rate of "one dean a month for the next 12 months." Kitchen's fellow professors thought it would be prudent to notify other research schools about Kitchen's murder.

Knox County Sheriff deputies placed a warning on the National Crime Information computer system that it was possible that a militant animal-rights group might be responsible for the Kitchen murder. In particular, it directed college deans across the country to be alert. Then they called in the FBI.

A few days later, United Press International reported that, according to investigators, Dr. Kitchen "had been very moderate in his dealings with the animal rights group, but no other possible motive could be established."

After learning that they were the subject of a nationwide alert, animal-rights organizations criticized the authorities for the action. Siriol Evans, spokeswoman for the 280,000-member People for the Ethical Treatment

Gate where Dr. Kitchen was murdered. *Author's collection.*

of Animals, located in Washington, D.C., said: "This whole thing is preposterous. Unfortunately, somebody is taking this tragic event and trying to turn it into a press opportunity against animal rights....This whole thing seems quite ridiculous because that type of action is completely against everything that the animal rights movement stands for."

Helen Mitternight of the Humane Society of the United States said, "I think it's incredibly irresponsible to name a group of people whose philosophy is non-violent as suspects because Knox County Sheriff's Department is stumped."

Animal researchers and industries immediately and forcefully repudiated the remarks by the animal rights spokeswomen, telling reporters that the animal rights people had burglarized laboratories and, "torched a multimillion-dollar research facility. They have sent furriers into economic shock, forced the withdrawal of untold thousands of dollars from federally funded experiments and compelled a growing number of companies to stop using animals to test for the safety of cosmetics and household products."

The *Los Angeles Times*, in describing the feud between the two sides, highlighted by the murder of Dr. Hyram Kitchen, wrote in 1990: "As animal advocates seek to turn what is still largely a protest movement into a long-term popular cause, they face a new and potentially devastating challenge. The animal-using industries and professions that have borne the brunt of the attacks (by members of the animal rights movement) have launched a massive, multimillion-dollar counteroffensive. The vitriol that is now building on both sides raises two questions: Have animal rights activists gone too far? And how far will their opponents go to stop them?"

The Fur Information Council of America spent more than $2 million on an advertising campaign. One ad read: "Today fur. Tomorrow leather. Then wool. Then meat….After that, medical research. Even circuses and zoos."

Edward Kavanaugh, president of the Cosmetic, Toiletry, and Fragrance Association, said: "We are in an escalating fight across the country….We are not dealing with rational opponents. We are dealing with zealots who cannot comprehend that a child's life is more important than a dog's."

The Knoxvillle, Tennessee news media reported in 1988 that the neighboring county of Loudon had agreed to furnish animals from its pound to Dr. Kitchen for his research pertaining to human diseases. Animal-rights advocates objected: "These cats and dogs might have become someone's pets." By the time of Kitchen's death, this arrangement had stopped.

The following excerpts from two articles written by Dr. Kitchen, with abundant use of medical terms, illustrate some of his research work, which compared some animal characteristics to those of humans.

Comparative Development Hematology: Animal Models to Study Human Fetal Erythropoiesis
A comparison of the ontogeny of hemoglobin is made in human, mouse and sheep. The difference and similarities are discussed to demonstrate the use of these animals as potential models to study regulation and transition of erythropoiesis during development. A general comparison of developmental erythropoiesis is made among various mammals with a discussion of how various mammals facilitate oxygen transport across the placenta by differing mechanisms.
—Hyram Kitchen, July 1976

Genetic and Structural Basis for Animal Hemoglobin Heterogeneity
The genetic and environmental basis of animal heterogeneity will be compared to and contrasted with the heterogeneity seen with the human hemoglobins and their abnormal forms. Animal hemoglobin heterogeneity due to multiple, polymorphic and abnormal hemoglobins will be illustrated.

The ontogeny of animal hemoglobin will be compared to the well established developmental sequence of the emergence of embryonic, fetal and adult hemoglobin in man. It is quite clear that in certain animal species the genetic basis of hemoglobin heterogeneity is limited to as few as three pairs of alleles for the various hemoglobin polypeptide chain types. In these examples only a single hemoglobin type may be prominent at any one stage of life. On the other hand, the great and remarkable degree of hemoglobin heterogeneity may be due to numerous duplications of genetic material.
—*Hyram Kitchen, December 1975*

Dr. D.J. Krahwinkel moved to the University of Tennessee from Michigan State University at the same time as Dr. Kitchen. He pointed with some pride toward some of the things they had accomplished at Michigan State. "We put birth controls in lions, performed caesarian sections on hyenas, and worked on giraffes. At the Detroit zoo, we sewed the trunk back on an elephant that had gotten into a fight. Dr. Kitchen was a pioneer. He did a lot of things that a lot of people only thought about doing."

Dr. Kitchen's widow said, "I wish I'd been in the car with him, that he and I didn't have to go through it alone." A few years after her husband's death, Mrs. Kitchen moved to Oregon.

David Davenport, chief of the Knox County Sheriff's Office Cold Case Investigative Unit, said: "In my mind it was someone close to him or someone close put a contract out on him, paid someone to do it. They definitely meant to kill him. This is just where somebody, it appears to be an execution, came up, bam, bam, bam, bam, no DNA that we could find, nothing that we can link back to someone."

Numerous people were interviewed, but no solid lead ever materialized. Davenport said in describing the investigation, "Every road you traveled met with a dead end."

4

THE MYSTERY SURROUNDING THE REDHEAD MURDERS

On April 24, 1985, twenty-six law enforcement officers from the FBI and the Tennessee Bureau of Investigation and agents from five states held an urgent meeting in Nashville, Tennessee, for the purpose of pooling information about a number of homicide victims found along highways in the Southeast. All of the victims were women, most were thought to be prostitutes and several had never been identified. Most of the victims had been strangled and their bodies dumped along the highways. Few clues were available, but the agencies agreed to work together and share information as they pursued leads. The murders were thought to have been committed from the late 1970s until 1992.

Throughout the investigation, it was suspected that the perpetrator was a truck driver, because the victims were nearly always found near an interstate highway. Eight of the homicides were strikingly similar. Most of the victims were redheads or had strawberry-blond hair, a trait that reporters had noticed. Believing it was beyond coincidence, reporters began calling the mysterious homicides the "Redhead Murders."

For thirty years after the urgent meeting in Nashville, no new leads involving the unknown victims were discovered. In 2018, one of the victims was finally identified by investigators. She was Tina Marie McKenney Farmer from Indianapolis, Indiana. She had been reported missing by her family in November 1984. She was found wrapped in a blanket near Jellico, Tennessee, on January 1, 1985. She was identified by matching fingerprints from her postmortem examination and those from an arrest in Indiana in

1983. After thirty-five years, investigators solved the case when Jerry Leon Johns was identified as her killer through DNA analysis. Johns, who died in prison in 2015, was also a suspect in other cases.

Also in 2018, DNA analysis established the identity of Espy Regina Black-Pilgrim from Spindale, North Carolina. Her body was discovered in an abandoned refrigerator in a dump off of U.S. Highway 258 in Knox County, Kentucky, in 1985. She had died of suffocation. The day before her body was discovered, she reportedly had been seen at a truck stop in Corbin, Kentucky, looking to find a ride to North Carolina. Interestingly, she had auburn-red hair. Because this murder and the murder of Tina Farmer occurred in such proximity, authorities strongly believed that the same person had committed both crimes. They theorized that the killer was constantly driving up and down the highways in the Southeast looking for his next victim.

As if the investigators were not busy enough, in March 1985, another victim was discovered, in Knoxville, Tennessee. Surprisingly, when this woman was found, she was still alive! Linda Schacke had been choked with a piece of her own T-shirt. Thinking she was deceased, the would-be killer dragged her into a storm drain underneath Interstate 40 in west Knoxville. The knot tied in the piece of material was similar to the one found around the neck of Tina Farmer, who had been killed two months earlier.

When Schacke recovered enough to be interviewed by the police, she implicated a truck driver from Cleveland, Tennessee. She told police that she went to a motel room with Jerry Leon Johns after she got off work at a local strip club. Later, she said, he told her that he was with the Texas Rangers and abducted her while holding a gun on her.

Johns was quickly picked up by authorities, who held out hope that this was the man responsible for the redhead murders. He was questioned about all of the roadside killings that had occurred in the last three years, but he denied any involvement in those cases.

A few days after his arrest, in an interview with the *Knoxville News-Sentinel*, Johns said: "Apparently I fit the mold of what they were looking for. You can't blame them. They've got a lot of unsolved cases all over the country. But they can try all they want, it won't work. I didn't do it."

Johns had been in jail almost a month in 1985 when the body identified as Black-Pilgrim was found in Kentucky. Investigators determined that she had been dead only a few days. A few weeks later, another unidentified woman's body was found just off of Interstate 81 in Greene County, Tennessee. She was about twenty years old and had red-tinted hair. Because he was in jail at the time of these murders, this, of course, meant that Johns was not the person authorities had been searching for regarding the redhead murders.

Johns, however, was charged for assaulting, kidnapping and leaving Linda Schacke for dead. He was convicted in a Knox County court and died in prison.

As the investigators continued working on the mysterious murders, they arrested another truck driver. When a redheaded woman escaped from the cab of a truck in Dyersburg, Tennessee, she implicated Thomas Lee Elkins. After extensive interviews, authorities found no evidence that Elkins had committed any of the crimes.

The closest law enforcement came to solving the redhead murders in the Southeast came after Sarah Nicole Hulbert was found dead in Nashville in 2007. An Illinois truck driver, Bruce Mendenhall, was arrested at a Nashville truck stop and charged with Hulbert's murder. He was also charged with the murder of an unidentified woman whose nude body was found in a garbage can in Lebanon, Tennessee, at about the same time.

Prosecutors described the cab of Mendenhall's truck as a "killing chamber." They discovered a rifle, handcuffs, a nightstick, latex gloves and a bag of women's clothing that contained DNA from five different women. He was convicted of the murder of the two victims found in the Nashville area, but investigators were never able to find evidence that he was responsible for the deaths of any of the other redheads.

For most of these victims, many of them prostitutes who hitchhiked from truck stop to truck stop, their murders will likely never be avenged. Former TBI Director Steve Watson said at the time: "A lot of them probably wouldn't even be reported missing. They're lost in society, and practically speaking, if they turn up missing, there's nobody to care."

5

THE MYSTERY THAT SWIRLED AROUND TRIPLE HOMICIDES IN OLIVER SPRINGS

The three-story mansion with its eighteen rooms that towered over the homes of the working-class citizens of Oliver Springs, Tennessee, seemed to be a bit out of place. It was built at the turn of the century by Joseph Richards, who made a fortune in the coal mining and railroad industries. The estate was located about thirty miles northwest of Knoxville, Tennessee. It covered six hundred acres and contained popular mineral springs.

Because the springs were thought to have healing powers, they were popular with people from several states and some foreign countries. To accommodate the large numbers of people visiting the springs, Richards also built a grand hotel with 150 rooms. Advertisements for the hotel boasted that it had electricity throughout the building, which was not common at that time.

Joseph Richards chose to will his estate to the members of his family who were still single. When they were all married, the estate was to be sold and the proceeds divided equally among his descendants. Ann, Margaret and Mary were unmarried and continued to live in the house for several years. Their brother Joseph had moved from the residence; Minnie, their older sibling, died when she was only sixteen years old.

Mayme Sienknecht, a married granddaughter of Joseph Richards, sued to have the will overturned. She lost to her cousins in a bitterly fought court case that continued for three years.

The Richards sisters with their mother. *Robbie Underwood.*

By 1940, Joseph had moved out, and his three sisters legally still made the mansion their home. Ann and Margaret did not work outside the home, but Mary taught school at Oliver Springs Elementary School.

The three sisters had made plans to see the new movie *Gone with the Wind*, and each had bought new dresses for the occasion. The ladies were fond of pretty clothes and set the fashion standard in their town. Maggie Wilson Thurmer, a piano student of Ann Richards who attended church with the sister, recalled years later: "They were always fashionably late. When they finally got there, they marched in dressed to the hilts."

On the cold morning of February 5, 1940, Mary asked two boys to take a note to her sisters, reminding them that they were to go see the movie at the Tennessee Theater in Knoxville that evening. The boys returned and reported that, after several knocks on the door, no one answered. Eight-year-old Tommy Diggs, one of the students, reported that he heard "funny noises" inside the house.

About the same time, Mrs. O.P. Jones was trying to bring something to the sisters and would later say that she got no answer when she knocked several times at the front and back doors. She said she heard the voices of two men inside the house and stressed that the voices were of two White men. She seemed to sense that something was wrong and said she was very concerned when she left.

Mary decided to send two more boys to deliver the same message to her sisters. When they returned, they told their teacher that no one answered their knocks; more alarming, they told her that through a basement window they saw the shadow of a man who appeared to be holding a lantern.

When Mary also learned that her sisters had not attended a scheduled missions meeting, she ran home in a state of panic. Entering the house through the kitchen door, Mary discovered Ann lying in a pool of blood. She ran out of the house screaming for help. It would be up to others to find the bodies of her other sister, Margaret, and their sixteen-year-old Black errand boy, Leonard "Powder" Brown.

Ann and Margaret Richards were buried on February 8, 1940, in the new dresses they had purchased to wear to see *Gone with the Wind*. Because of the stirrings of racial unrest that had rapidly spread among the populace, there was no funeral for Leonard Brown, and he was secretly buried in an unmarked grave. Rumors were rampant that the Ku Klux Klan threatened to drag his body through the streets of Oliver Springs.

Anderson County sheriff Robert Smith quickly stated that it appeared to be a murder-suicide. He said, "The Negro boy must have killed the sisters and then turned the gun on himself." This brought about an immediate uproar from many in Oliver Springs. Those who knew the victims argued that the sheriff's statement could not possibly be correct. After all, the sheriff had been unable to explain the several cigarette butts left at the head of the stairs, at a perfect location for a lookout post. Further, they pointed out that Leonard Brown had no powder marks or burns on his hands.

Investigators learned from those who knew Leonard Brown that he was very timid and was scared of the noise made by firecrackers and guns. They were told that Leonard would turn as pale as ashes when he was scared. This, they said, was how he had acquired the nickname "Powder."

A few days later, a coroner's inquisition jury learned that Ann Richards had been shot in the head and her sister Margaret had been shot in the head and throat. Leonard Brown was shot between the eyes from such a downward angle, the coroner explained to the jury, that it would have been impossible for him to have taken his own life in the manner suggested by the sheriff. In the meantime, the townspeople asked, "How could a man who was so scared of firearms and with no training with weapons have fired the gun so accurately?"

Most of the twenty-eight witnesses who testified at the inquisition did not believe that Sheriff Smith's opinion was correct. A decision was reached in just twenty minutes that rebuffed the sheriff's theory. The jury decided that the three victims had "met their deaths at the hands of parties unknown."

A thorough investigation was then started. Authorities made a list of people they thought could possibly have a motive for committing the triple homicide. In the first few days, the names of several people emerged, and multiple theories were put forth.

It was learned that several prejudiced citizens resented the Richards sisters' showing benevolence toward members of the small Black population. They often hired them for work in and around their house. The investigators were also told that Powder Brown had recently become angry when he thought the suit the sisters had bought for him was not as nice as the one that they bought for one of his friends. Some said that this was possibly the motive. Hardly anyone believed this to be the motive.

A few days before the murders occurred, two convicts had been released from Brushy Mountain State Penitentiary, about eighteen miles away, and had arrived at the Oliver Springs bus station, which was located near the mansion. For a short time, they found themselves on the suspect list. They were removed from the list, however, when the investigators were reminded of Mrs. Jones's adamant testimony that the voices were of White men. The former convicts were Black men.

Mrs. Jones was quoted in a 1940 edition of the *Knoxville News-Sentinel* as follows: "It was shortly after noon, and I went to the back door. I knocked and knocked and knocked but couldn't get an answer. Then I went to the front door, still no answer so I listened. I heard inside the house the voices of two men talking low like. I know they were men, White men at that."

Some thought that Jones stressed that she remembered that the men were White out of fear that some in town might be tempted to take the law into their own hands regarding the two strangers. If nothing else, with law enforcement officials desperate to find suspects, without Jones's testimony they could have easily been falsely accused.

A family named Hannah lived next door to the Richards, and it was learned that the murder weapon had been stolen from their house. The Hannahs and the Richards were in a dispute over a property line at the time.

Some bootleggers came under the scrutiny of the investigators. It was said that the murdered sisters had found some whiskey that the bootleggers had stored in their Presbyterian Church basement and reported it to the authorities. Some thought that the sisters were killed as retaliation for snitching.

The name of the Richards sisters' cousin, Mamie Sienknecht, was put on the suspect list. It was she, after all, with whom they had had such a bitter inheritance court fight just a few years earlier. In many people's minds, she had the strongest motive of all.

Even though citizens of Oliver Springs still talk of the horrendous triple murder, the trail in 1940 soon grew cold. It seemed that everyone had a theory. In some cases, residents openly accused the person(s) they felt sure were guilty. But the authorities could never come up with enough evidence to bring charges against anyone.

Then, in 2001, it appeared that the pieces of the puzzle were finally falling into place and the long-ago mystery might be solved. Several people in Oliver Springs were excited at the news; others appeared to be worried and wished the whole thing would just go away. The latter feared that the names of their families might be dragged through an awful scandal.

Sixty years after the murders, a gentleman came back to Oliver Springs asking if two particular local men were still alive. He said these men threatened him with his life when he saw them near the Richards house the day before the murder. He thought they killed the Richards sisters and would not hesitate to kill him, so he quickly left town.

When the gentleman was assured that the two men were deceased, he told his story implicating the two men. Television, radio and newspaper reporters came to cover the breaking of the unsolved murder mystery. For a few days, they ran stories that included the names of the accused men, but when the men's families threatened lawsuits, the stories abruptly stopped. The mystery was likely solved, but the authorities and the news media went silent. The

The belated grave marker of Leonard "Powder" Brown. *Robbie Underwood.*

accused perpetrators were no longer alive, so the authorities decided that to pursue it any longer would serve no purpose. For the same reason, the names of the accused will not be passed along in this publication.

In 2015, former Oliver Springs resident Danita Ashley wrote a book, *Murder by the Springs*. After conducting extensive research, she wrote that it was obvious that "whoever committed the murders had a deep hatred for Ann and Margaret. Powder Brown was just at the wrong place at the wrong time."

With the case unofficially solved, Brown was finally cleared. In 2001, after sixty-one years, Leonard "Powder" Brown was given a funeral and a grave marker. Betty Shelton, cousin of the slain Richards sisters, organized the funeral and paid for the marker. Shelton said, "I was proud to see Powder Brown cleared and to have a memorial service for him."

6
MAYHEM IN THE GREAT SMOKY MOUNTAINS

The Great Smoky Mountains National Park covers 522,000 acres of the Appalachian Mountains. Elevations in the park range between 800 and 6,643 feet above sea level. In 1934, the Rockefeller family furnished most of the $11 million required for the purchase of the land.

The area chosen has the highest peaks east of the Mississippi River. Hundreds of miles of hiking trails with occasional shelters, spectacular waterfalls and numerous campsites offer an appeal to all outdoor enthusiasts. Because of this, the park has become the most visited of all national parks.

For the millions who visit each year, lifelong memories of their experiences remain. Unfortunately, for a few, their experiences tell a different story, as the following events illustrate.

WHAT HAPPENED TO DENNIS MARTIN?

Spence Field in the Great Smoky Mountains, a popular destination at 4,900 feet, is reached by the moderately difficult Anthony Creek Trail. From the parking lot in Cades Cove to Spence Field, the hiker must cover a little more than five miles, but the reward is spectacular views of the mountain on the North Carolina side of the park. In June, blooming mountain laurel is abundant. White and pink flowers seem to be everywhere.

Spence Field was a favorite camping location for the Martin family. On Friday, June 13, 1969, William Martin, a Knoxville, Tennessee architect, took his father, Clyde Martin, and two sons, Douglas and Dennis, on a camping trip in the mountains. That night, they camped in Russell Field, and the next morning, they started the two-and-one-half-mile hike east to Spence Field. There was a hiking shelter there, and rain was expected.

At about 4:00 p.m. on June 14, the Martin brothers and two boys they had met from Alabama were playing around the shelter while William and others watched them. In a few minutes, Douglas and the two Alabama boys came to the shelter, but Dennis was not with them. William Martin became concerned, and within two minutes, he and other adults started searching for the missing Dennis.

The searchers were concerned that Dennis had become confused and might have found a trail that headed down the mountain and away from Spence Field. It was decided that all the searchers except William would carefully search Spence Field. William hiked the trail to and from Russell Field, where they had camped the previous night. None of the searchers located seven-year-old Dennis Martin.

View from the top of the Smoky Mountains. *Daniel and Carolyn Harrison.*

Mr. and Mrs. Terry Chilcoat arrived at the shelter about the time it was discovered that Dennis was missing. They reported that they had come up the Bote Mountain Trail but had not seen Dennis.

With the Martins now in a state of panic, Dennis's grandfather Clyde Martin decided to hike down the Anthony Creek Trail in an effort to get help. When he arrived at Cades Cove at 8:00 p.m., he quickly found Park Ranger Larry Nielson. Nielson immediately notified the National Park Service and asked for assistance. He then started hiking up the trail toward Spence Field with the grandfather.

Halfway up the mountain, darkness accompanied by a thunderstorm with heavy lightning made their travel extremely difficult. At this time, the grandfather, nearing exhaustion, noticed an alarming sudden drop in temperature. The official temperature in the mountains for that June night was fifty degrees Fahrenheit.

Responding to Ranger Nielson's call for help, several rangers converged on Spence Field during the night. The heavy rain continued as the rangers searched, sometimes on their hands and knees. The two inches of rain that fell during the night had swollen all streams in the area, and this complicated the rangers' search.

National Park Ranger Dwight McCarter, who joined the search early on Sunday morning, wrote the following in his journal:

> *I just finished reading the paper and was watching and listening to the storm for over an hour when the telephone rings. The call is from Chief Ranger Snedden who tells me about the Martin boy and asks me to report for duty tomorrow at 5:00 A.M. at the Bote Mountain Trail. I do not say to him, but I know the rain storm is a major complication to the search, greatly diminishing the chances of finding Dennis. There is a serious risk of exposure and hypothermia for the boy. The rain will wash out whatever tracking sign we might have been able to find, rendering the use of tracking dogs all but useless. I set my alarm for an early rise, but that turns out to be a joke. Sleep is first elusive and then fitful when it finally comes.*
>
> *I am up before the alarm goes off and at the rendezvous early, assigned as a member of a four-man search crew going to Spence. Getting there is a problem. Although there are nine jeeps and three trucks available today, every jeep we can find is already in use to shuttle searchers up to Spence. The last mile or so near the top is the worst problem because each vehicle headed up meets others coming down and*

there are few places to pass. Over 2.5 inches of rain fell last night in the storm. All of the streams are up and very turbulent with most over their banks. The trail-road up Bote Mountain is in bad shape with running water, mud and washouts everywhere.

Although the night search had not yielded a single clue, the rangers did their best to console the family members, telling them that even though Dennis would be wet and cold, he would likely survive the ordeal. The next morning, the rangers established a base for continuing the search at Spence Field. Because the heavy rain had made most of the trails difficult to negotiate, a helicopter was secured that could bring additional searchers and supplies up the mountain. A massive search was about to begin.

Over the years, National Park Service personnel had learned to allow only experienced, well-conditioned searchers to participate in searches that took place in such a harsh and dangerous environment. Therefore, the first searchers were park rangers, park maintenance employees, members of the Smoky Mountain Hiking Club, two area rescue squads and a few select experienced hikers. By 10:00 a.m. on Sunday, June 15, one hundred searchers started combing the area where Dennis was last seen.

At the same time on Sunday morning, the Martins' pastor was notified that Dennis was missing and a search had begun. When Violet Martin, Dennis's mother, arrived at their church, Reverend George Ambrister had to break the news to her. She and several other church members immediately left for the search site. They arrived there at noon.

Roads leading into the area were so clogged by the cars of people coming to help in the search that rangers were forced to block all traffic. Approximately 150 additional experienced hikers, after being screened by rangers, were allowed to pass through and were immediately assigned areas to search.

Residents of nearby Townsend, Tennessee, brought food and drinks to the ranger station in Cades Cove. The Red Cross set up a camp at the search site and brought ample food, water and blankets. The searchers would be well supplied throughout the days of the search.

Heavy rain returned to the mountains late in the day on Sunday. The effort by the 250 searchers had to be suspended until the following morning, if the weather allowed. When darkness fell, not a single clue of Dennis was found.

Monday, the following day, was clear, and fifty more searchers were chosen from hundreds of volunteers to join the search. A heliport was built that would allow the helicopter to land safely when supplies were brought to the top of the mountain. Five dogs with their handlers joined the search operation. By the end of the day, the original searchers were exhausted and told to go home and get some rest. They were replaced by members of the National Guard and several more experienced hikers.

On Tuesday, the number of searchers was 365. All remained hopeful, but some started talking of the possibility that Dennis had become the victim of a bear or a wild boar.

Spirits were temporarily lifted late on Tuesday when a report came through on a park ranger's radio: "The little boy has been found." Hopes were dashed, however, when it was determined that the little boy referred to on the radio was a boy who had been missing only a short time while fishing with his grandfather in another part of the mountains.

On Wednesday, the number of searchers had incredibly grown to 615. The search coordinator realized that most of the organization had now broken down but knew that time was running out and perhaps someone out of this large number might be able to turn up a clue.

By Thursday, many more searchers were completely exhausted and forced to take themselves off the mountain. They were replaced by 690 fresh searchers who continued to check every inch of the immediate area. Still, no clues were found.

William Martin was taken up in a helicopter and tried calling out Dennis's name by loudspeaker, but the noise of the helicopter's engine was so great that William could not be heard.

Realizing that the situation had now become desperate, hundreds of volunteers were showing up every day intending to help find the lost little boy. Many became irate when they were turned away by the park officials, who still insisted that searchers had to be experienced mountain hikers. They were sure that chaos would have resulted if everyone were turned loose in the rugged and dangerous mountains.

The situation had become a public relations nightmare for the park service. Pressure became more intense because of daily calls from the governor's mansion in Nashville and the White House in Washington, D.C. Articles about the massive search appeared in most newspapers around the country. Television stations often broke into their regularly scheduled programs to give progress reports on the search.

After five days had passed and no signs of Dennis had been found, National Park Service officials were forced to tell the parents that it was now becoming less likely by the hour that they would be able to find their son.

Bramble at the edge of a field similar to the one that searchers faced each morning. *Daniel and Carolyn Harrison.*

The parents and the hundreds of searchers were distraught at this news, but they already knew this was the case.

Desperate to keep the searchers and newspaper reporters from giving up on the search for her son, Dennis's mother wrote the following heartrending note to several newspapers in the Southeast: "Dennis begs to go to the mountains on weekends. He is an experienced mountain hiker for a seven-year-old, and is usually out in front of the group, picking up the trail. Please publish this photograph of Dennis and ask anyone who might see a child fitting his description, and perhaps seeming to be 'out of place,' to please contact us or the police."

Several theories were discussed by searchers and people at home. In addition to concerns that Dennis had encountered bears or boars, the possibility of kidnapping seemed to be the only plausible explanation left for the boy's disappearance. With this in mind, the Martins requested that the National Park Service call in the FBI. This was done immediately. This agency, too, had little to go on and ultimately found no evidence that a kidnapping had occurred.

Throughout the sixth day of the search, heavy thunderstorms raked the area. In spite of the intolerant weather, 780 searchers spent the day looking for any trace of Dennis. With so many volunteers showing up every day, a couple of newspaper articles pointed out that Tennesseans were certainly living up to their nickname, the "Volunteers."

On the seventh day, Saturday, fourteen hundred searchers, now desperate, went back over ground that had already been covered on previous days. The area that had been thoroughly searched now totaled nearly fifteen square miles, an area the little boy could not possibly have gone beyond on his own.

On Sunday, day eight of the search, the number of searchers had declined to one thousand. Ranger McCarter wrote of what he saw:

> *A roadblock has been established at the forks of the Little River/Townsend "Y" at 5:00 A.M. today to keep park visitors out of the search area and to control the large numbers of volunteers which are expected today. We travel by bus up Laurel Creek Road to Cades Cove where two Chinook helicopters and four other smaller choppers are airlifting searchers to the mountain helispots. I have never seen anything like this before. With the large number of military, park, and volunteer civilian searchers, and all of the vehicles and equipment to service them, it looks like either an invasion is being launched or an evacuation is underway. Many volunteers are agitated because they have to wait hours for transportation, first at the "Y" then at the helispots and other transfer points. Many never get to the search area.*

On Monday, the number of searchers was 427. Because of intermittent heavy rain, the searchers were forced to stay in their tents most of the day. Ranger McCarter recorded:

> *We are "dog tired" from only getting a few hours sleep for many days and hiking strenuously up and down hill all day long with little rest. There is, of course, a sense of great urgency to try to find Dennis. A little boy could survive on green apples or roots or even no food at all for a week or so as long as he has water. There seems to be no lack of that commodity. If he has been able to find shelter from the many cold rain storms and could stay relatively dry, he could be alive and maybe not even in dire straits. However, time and search possibilities are running out and we all know that after ten days, the likelihood of a tragic end to this search is growing more likely.*

With the weather improving on Tuesday, 482 searchers showed up for work. On Wednesday, the number was 403. Then, the National Park Service announced that it had no choice but to reduce the size of the search. Also, the reduced search would be suspended in three more days if Dennis had not been found. Beyond that, a limited search would continue for sixty days. At that point, the search would officially end.

Even though hope of finding Dennis Martin was now essentially gone, on Thursday, 121 searchers showed up. The number for Friday was 68. On Saturday, 196 searchers came. Sunday brought 318 and the end of the intense search. The somber searchers who were still present watched Park Rangers start removing their equipment from their base camp.

The limited search was conducted by three rangers who had been raised in the Smoky Mountains and were thoroughly familiar with the search area. J.R. Buchanan, Arthur Whitehead and Grady Whitehead searched for approximately sixty more days.

Dennis's family offered a $5,000 reward for information that might lead to his safe return. The reward was never claimed.

A MASS MURDERER DISAPPEARS IN THE GREAT SMOKY MOUNTAINS NATIONAL PARK

Several people noticed that a rusty-brown Chevrolet with Maryland license plates had been sitting in the parking lot near to the starting point of Jakes Creek Trail for about two weeks. On March 18, 1976, Roy Ownby called the office of the Great Smoky Mountains National Park Rangers to report his concern. Ranger C.E. Hinrichs was sent to investigate.

Even though everything inside the car appeared to be normal, Hinrichs radioed his dispatcher to run a check on the license plate. In less than a minute, he received a startling reply. He was advised to use extreme caution, because the driver of that car was a wanted mass murderer who was likely armed and dangerous.

The ranger called the FBI office in Knoxville, Tennessee, and within two hours, agents arrived and took control of the investigation. When they searched the car, they found men's clothing, a shotgun and shells, dog biscuits and blankets covered with blood.

The FBI agents knew very well who the driver of the car was. They had been alerted to be on the lookout for William Bradford Bishop Jr., who was wanted for murder in Maryland. The FBI agents told the rangers all they knew about Bishop and the crimes he was accused of committing. Their story started with the discovery of five partly burned bodies in a shallow grave near Columbia, North Carolina. They had been soaked with gasoline. It appeared to the investigators that three children and two adults were in the hastily dug grave. A shovel still lay a few feet away. It appeared that all five victims had died from a blow to the head by a blunt object.

Meanwhile, the neighbors in an upscale neighborhood in Bethesda, Maryland, contacted the police during the first week of March 1976, because they saw no activity around the Bishop house, and newspapers were piling up in the driveway. It was not like the Bishops to leave for an extended time without letting the neighbors know and without stopping delivery of their newspapers. The neighbors said that William Bradford Bishop Jr., age thirty-nine, lived there with his wife, Annette (thirty-seven); his mother, Lobelia (sixty-eight); and sons William Bradford III (fourteen), Brenton (ten) and Geoffrey (five).

The police entered the Bishop house and found blood in several rooms. It was obvious to the police that violent struggles had taken place in multiple rooms. After autopsies were completed in North Carolina, the bodies were positively identified as members of William Bishop's family. He immediately became suspect number one.

Bishop certainly did not fit the mold of a mass murderer. He was a graduate of Yale University and had earned his master's degree in Italian from Middlebury College in Vermont. From all appearances, he had been a successful employee with the U.S. Diplomatic Corps, where he negotiated trade agreements with several countries.

The neighbors said that Bishop always seemed relaxed and easygoing. Few, if any, knew that he was prone to violent outbursts of temper or that he suffered from chronic amnesia. None knew that he took antidepressant medication and was under the constant care of a psychiatrist.

The FBI learned that the violent actions by Bishop were precipitated by his being passed over for a promotion he was expecting to get. Co-workers reported that Bishop started complaining of flu-like symptoms and went home early that day.

The FBI also discovered that Bishop had stopped on his way home at a hardware store and bought a hammer and a gasoline can. He stopped at a service station and filled the can with gasoline. He stopped at his bank and withdrew several hundred dollars. He bought a shovel from a hardware store in Potomac, Maryland.

Bishop used the newly purchased hammer to bludgeon to death the five members of his family, carried them to his station wagon, called his golden retriever and headed south. The next time he was spotted was in Jacksonville, North Carolina, when he used a credit card to buy shoes from a sporting-goods store. Witnesses reported that a woman walked his dog while he was buying the shoes. The police were never able to identify this person.

Once they had been briefed by the FBI, the Great Smoky Mountains park rangers were asked to give as much assistance to the federal agents as possible to track down the killer. Ranger Hinrichs promised that they would help provide support as needed.

Knowing that Bishop could still be in the park, the FBI agents requested help from the best trackers and search dogs the rangers could furnish. The park service provided the services of their most experienced backcountry rangers, Bill Burke, J.R. Buchanan, Jack Collier, Dwight McCarter and Lennie Garver. Among the search dogs brought in by the FBI were two German shepherds that had participated in the searches for Patty Hearst and Jimmy Hoffa. For several days, a helicopter circled over the area.

On March 19, 1976, twenty-five heavily armed FBI agents, working in conjunction with park rangers, began a search in the area that surrounded the Elkmont community. Elkmont was the only remaining area to have U.S. government–issued permits to operate cabins within a national park.

As soon as the dogs arrived, one quickly picked up Bishop's trail, which led directly to the front door of one of the cabins. The dog could not be moved from the cabin until the agents thoroughly searched the premises. They found nothing, but the strong scent that the dogs had picked up so quickly made them think that Bishop had been there recently. It was assumed that Bishop had fled into the high mountains.

On March 20, rangers closed every trail that led into the rugged backcountry. Every hiker coming out of the mountain was interviewed. Several hikers reported that they had in fact seen Bishop earlier in the day. However, leads started coming in from so many places in the mountain that it became obvious that these interviews were suspect.

Heavy rains, which are so common in the Smoky Mountains, moved in and obliterated any scent that the dogs might have been able to follow. Since the large number of FBI agents and park rangers had combed the area around Elkmont and found nothing, the search was ended.

Most of the searchers believed that Bishop hiked deep into the mountains and took his own life. They reasoned that he likely found himself in a more rational frame of mind and, faced with the reality of his evil actions, took the easy way out.

Newlyweds and a Suicide Pact

Since the inception of Gatlinburg and the Great Smoky Mountains National Park, they have been a favorite honeymoon location for thousands of couples. Most take pictures that they will keep and treasure for the rest of their lives. This is what makes the following story of a young couple so tragically different.

At 7:15 p.m. on Sunday, March 29, 1981, a young lady wearing a blood-spattered lavender party dress arrived at the Ranger Station at Abrams Creek. Ranger Bill Webb noted that her slashed wrist was at odds with her rather neat appearance. The ranger asked if she was alone, and she answered ominously, "I am now."

Janet Rudd told a rambling story about herself and her new husband—a story that had begun when they met at South Florida University in Tampa. She said that she had married John Rudd in secret a few days earlier, on March 5, in Bradenton, Florida. They immediately began planning to disappear together in the Smoky Mountains. They reasoned that if they simply disappeared, no one would grieve over them.

While this conversation was going on, Ranger Lowell Higgins at Ranger Headquarters received a call from a John Rudd Sr., who was trying to locate his missing son. His son had told some friends in Florida that he was planning to visit the Smoky Mountains. Given this information, Ranger Webb surmised that the bloodied young lady who had shown up at the ranger station was Mr. Rudd's daughter-in-law. Park rangers immediately started an investigation.

Ranger Higgins remembered that he had talked with this couple a week earlier at the Abrams Creek Trail parking lot. When he drove up, they were standing beside a Volkswagen Beetle and were wearing backpacks. They said they were going to hike to the Abrams Creek area and camp there for four nights. Because it was 7:00 p.m., and they had a five-mile hike ahead of them, Higgins persuaded them to stay there in the Cades Cove campground and begin their hike in the morning. The ranger remembered that they followed his advice and did not leave for Abrams Creek until 2:00 p.m. the next day.

About the same time, Janet's mother received a letter from her daughter that was postmarked Knoxville, Tennessee, on March 22. Janet told her mother that she and her new husband were headed for Canada and that she would like for her father to come and take her car back to Florida. John Rudd mailed a letter to his parents, telling them that he and his new bride were going to Peru.

Ranger Webb could see that although there was a superficial cut on Janet's wrist, it was not serious, and she was capable of answering questions. He asked her, "Were you beside a stream?" She answered, "No, streams are cold." He asked about her husband, "Did he fall?" She answered, "No, he didn't fall." She said that she and John had abandoned their camping gear along the trail.

After several more questions, Janet blurted out, "He took his own life. That is what he wanted." When the ranger looked puzzled, she went on to explain that shortly after she had met John, they had started planning a suicide pact!

Janet said that on that particular morning, March 29, 1981, John told her that he was going for a walk and left their camp. After a while, she went to search for him and found him bleeding profusely from razor-blade cuts on his wrist.

She said that John's skin was cold to the touch and the large amount of blood made her sick. Then, remembering the pact they had agreed to, she said she started cutting her wrist, and the pain was so great that she was unable to cut any deeper. She told the ranger that at that point she decided she would find a less painful way to join John "on the other side."

By 2:00 a.m. on March 30, several rangers had gathered at the ranger station, and they decided that a search for John would be started at dawn by retracing Janet's trail. Unfortunately, that morning, a heavy rain came and completely erased Janet's footprints.

Janet was taken to the University of Tennessee Hospital, where her wrist required six stitches. The attending physician said that if her husband's wounds were somewhat similar to Janet's, he might still be alive. The rangers took Janet back to the Abrams Creek Ranger Station, where she ate a large meal and promptly went to sleep.

At daylight on March 30, the FBI and tracking dogs joined the search with employees of the National Park Service. A U.S. Army National Guard helicopter from the nearby McGhee-Tyson Air Base also joined the search.

At about 4:00 p.m., the National Guard crew spotted what appeared to be an abandoned tent along the trail on Polecat Ridge, approximately two miles from the Abrams Creek Ranger Station. They agreed to stay over the scene until the searchers could get there.

According to Janet's statement, the tent that the helicopter was hovering over was at the couple's next-to-last campsite. She said that John should be found close to a brown blanket that would mark their last campsite.

Just before dark, the searchers found the second and final campsite. John was not found there, and with darkness closing in, the search would have to be resumed the following morning.

Janet's mother and father arrived from Florida, and Janet was released to their care. She agreed to return to the ranger station the next morning to assist in the search.

At 6:45 a.m. on Tuesday, March 31, a search team went as far as possible up Rabbit Creek Trail by jeep. Continuing on foot, at 8:30 a.m., the team found a brown blanket, soap and several razor blades. They were sure they had found the campsite that Janet had described. This site was only about a quarter of a mile from the first campsite. This morning, John's parents arrived from Florida.

The immediate area was thoroughly searched all day, and John was not found. Ranger Higgins reported later that Janet's story kept changing, and it was becoming apparent that something was wrong. John was clearly not where she said he would be found. It was now obvious that if John had moved to another location, he had been alive when Janet left him. The search again ended with darkness.

In the early morning on April 1, Janet accompanied the searchers as they again searched the forest for her husband. Higgins, observing Janet closely, noticed that she had become more composed than she was when she first reported the incident.

Janet said, "If he was here, you would have found him. He was very near here." When she stared in one direction for a while, she was asked if John was in that direction. She answered, "No, he's back in the other way." The rangers were becoming suspicious that she was trying to confuse them. They agreed that she probably did not want them to find her husband.

While the searchers went about their work, Rangers Higgins and Webb continued talking with Janet in an attempt to gather some background information. She told them that even though she and John had never been in love, they both shared a dream of dying in an unusually beautiful place. They thought it would be nice to be married when they died.

She said that once they left their car in the Cades Cove parking lot, they had navigated by using a map from the *Hiker's Guide to the Smokies*. She said that they were completely out of food when they reached their final campsite near Scott Gap.

At 2:30 p.m., one of the search teams found John Rudd's body. It was about one-half mile from the couple's last campsite. He was lying on his back, and four deep lacerations were noticeable on his left wrist. The searchers thought that John had cut his wrist near the nearby stream and then moved under a fallen tree to be out of the heavy rain that was falling at the time. Because of the blood trail and John's tracks in the area, they theorized that when the rain stopped, he had moved about ten feet to the spot where he was found. Ranger Higgins thought that it was likely that John had lived several hours after his wrist had been cut.

Before John Rudd's body was taken to the University of Tennessee Hospital in Knoxville, his father identified his body at the Abrams Creek Ranger Station. Janet accompanied her parents back to Florida.

7

THE TRAGIC WARTIME EXPERIENCE
OF CAPTAIN THOMAS DRINNEN

When you go home,
Tell them of us, and say,
For your tomorrow,
We gave our today.
—Patrick O'Donnell, *Into the Rising Sun*

By 1943, much of the world had been fighting for upward of four years in what would later be called World War II. For several countries, their civilians as well as their military personnel experienced the fog of war on their very doorsteps. American civilians held some comfort in knowing that the heavy fighting, at least for the time being, was separated from them by an ocean.

When the hostilities began, Japan and Germany were already experiencing gasoline shortages. The U.S government, in something of a disinformation campaign, made it be known that gasoline was in short supply in this country as well. Actually, gasoline remained in fairly good supply throughout the war. The commodity shortage that came close to being an Achilles' heel was rubber. This was the result of Japan seizing most of the rubber plantations in the South Pacific.

Much was made of the tight rationing of gasoline (three gallons per week for most), but this was mainly a way of forcing a reduction in driving, thereby preserving precious rubber. Interestingly, chemists at Tennessee Eastman's plant in Kingsport, Tennessee, developed a synthetic rubber that civilians could use. With this breakthrough, most of the available natural rubber could be provided to the military.

Another shortage, as in any war, was that of doctors trained to treat the types of injuries common on the battlefield. In the 1940s, long before specialists were commonplace, nearly all doctors were general practitioners. On entering the service and completing basic training, doctors were given the rank of captain and sent to a facility to learn the procedures that would be needed to treat the traumatic battlefield injuries they were certain to see.

Doctor Thomas Drinnen had been practicing medicine for nine years in Knoxville, Tennessee, when he was drafted. His induction into the army was not typical. For most potential draftees, having three small sons would exempt them from serving in the military. At that time, however, the shortage of well-trained doctors was too acute for this general rule to apply to Dr. Drinnen.

Thomas Brabson Drinnen and Trula Fern Brooks were lifelong sweethearts; they never dated anyone else. After high school, Fern went to a business college in Knoxville, and Tom went to the University of Tennessee. After graduating, he went to the University of Tennessee's School of Medicine in Memphis. Fern occasionally visited Tom there, and in 1932, during one of her visits, they went to Arkansas and got married. They lived in Memphis until he graduated the following year.

After Tom's internship in St. Louis, they moved back to Knoxville and bought a house in the Holston Hills area. Tom began practicing medicine as a general practitioner and obstetrician. His two older boys remember riding along with their father as he made house calls. His office was in the Medical Arts Building in Knoxville.

In 1942, Tom was inducted into the army and sent to basic training at Fort Rucker in Alabama. From there, he went to Memphis and the Kennedy Army Hospital for specialized trauma training and then was assigned to the Forty-Eighth Army General Hospital Unit. Fern and their three boys were with Tom in Memphis the day he learned he would be shipping out for England. She and the boys returned to Knoxville for the duration of his deployment.

Captain Drinnen's outfit caught a train bound for New York on December 15, 1943. In New York, they boarded an old French ship that was to take them to England. The first day at sea, the vessel caught fire and had to return to port. It was then declared to be unseaworthy. The unit would be in New York two weeks longer as it awaited assignment to another ship.

Drinnen received a letter from his mother while waiting in New York. The letter showed her concern for her son, who was on his way to war. She closed with, "So write where and as often as you can—as I dearly love you son and pray for you each day and am sure God will take care of you."

A few days before Christmas, Tom received a wire from Fern telling him that his mother had suffered a stroke and died. His request to come home from New York for her funeral was denied.

Tom boarded the steamship HMS *Queen Elizabeth* for the transatlantic crossing. When he first reached southern England in January 1944, he looked up Cecil Frazier, an army chaplain who was married to Tom's sister Margaret. Soon after landing in England, Captain Drinnen and Captain Moore were ordered to the small town of Swindon in Wiltshire. The roommates were billeted in the private home of Percy and Nell Mitchell.

He wrote to Fern just about every day that he was separated from his family, and the following excerpts from some of the letters show how he tried to be husband and father from far away.

> *Dear Fern:*
> *Just received your wire about mother—needless to say it hit hard and low, but that's the way things go at times. Give me all the details about the funeral and tell Anna to write me any details. Sorry I'm unable to attend, but this is also out of my control and nothing I can say about it except to say I can't attend.*
> *P.S. Fern, you have my power of attorney and can sit for me legally in any capacity. I hope things can be arranged and not sell the farm as it is good security for old age for any of us, should we, any of us, become disabled. At least it will give 3 meals a day and it's gradually getting more and more out of debt.*
>
> *Sunday, December 26, 1943*
> *Dear Fern and Boys:*
> *(Fern: Read this part to the boys)*
> *Danny boy, did you get a toy gun for Christmas? What about a rocky horse? Tommy and Gary, daddy wants both of you to write me and tell me how you liked Christmas and what you got....Daddy sure missed being with you and mother and let's just hope we can be together again before next Christmas. Be good boys and remember to take your vitamin pills.*
> *Love,*
> *Tom*

Monday afternoon:
I realize the worry mother had helped a lot toward inducing that last attack that got her. It's all beyond my control, so I try not to think about it, but it's still hard to think I had anything to do with the fatal attack…I know boys are having a big time, just keep them in line and make them mind so they'll grow up to be fine young men.…Give all three a big kiss for me and love to you sweetheart.
Love,
Tom

Tuesday
Goodness how I miss you and the boys, I think about how Danny would talk on going to bed and the romps the boys had. Well we'll have more of the same—and the sooner the better.
All my love,
Tom

Sunday Night—January 16, 1944
I wrote the boys yesterday, see if they won't write me. I know they'll soon forget at that age they have a daddy unless you take pains to impress on them each day where I am. Show them the picture and let them remember how I look, and point out on the map where I am. Keep telling them I'll be back when war's over.…
Love,
Tom

January 26, 1944
…Sorry to hear Danny [is] *still having trouble with his ear. Don't hesitate to take him back for Ed to check and be careful about the sulfadiazine also. If he doesn't look just right have one of baby men or McAlwaine see him.…I don't know why I tell you such things, I know you'll take care of them.…*
Love,
Tom

January 30, 1944
Dearest Wife and Boys:
I sure miss getting up on Sunday mornings and reading the Sunday morning paper in bed with Danny Boy and those two rascals, Gary and Tommy.

Then go have some scrambled eggs or hot cakes or biscuits. My, that was real enjoyment and how I realize it now. Here I'm up at 7 a.m. (that's 1 and ½ hours before daylight). It's cold, damp, make fires one day each week. What a life.
All my love,
Tom

February 6, 1944
To Boys:
…Now all three of you kiss mother for me. Have you? Well, do it again and make it pop real hard. Have you?—Now that's better—Bye now and write me again.
Love to all,
Daddy

February 13, 1944
Dearest Fern:
Time marches on and today new changes came about and always mean more work for the few of us who always do the duty details. Letters will be irregular for a few days, then, things will settle down again.…Worked until 7:30 last night.…Fern I wish I could be with you and the boys today. My how I love you and miss you and those rascals. Take good care of the boys and of yourself and always remember I am yours, only yours and with love, and all of it to the sweetest, dearest wife in the world.
Love,
Tom

February 20, 1944
Dear Fern:
…I got up and went to church at 11:00—yes me. In fact I go about every Sunday. Heard a preacher from London, big Baptist, and enjoyed it very much. Nell and Percy are a fine couple, no children, about 40 I would suppose.…
Love,
Tom

In the following letter, which would be his final one, Captain Drinnen was almost prophetic as he described the primitive gas water heater they were using.

Wednesday Night—February 23, 1944
…The bath room is cold as the devil—no heat at all…no running hot water in any of the houses. They heat water with what they call geysers, looks like old still, very primitive, but suits them.…Very little coal and no heat until afternoon or evening.…Funny even in this cold, birds are singing, grass is green and pretty flowers—daffodils are in full bloom now.…Hope you get the bonds for boys—I can't find anything for them—They'll never know and I believe they will be happy for them. Anxious to get the pictures of the sweetest family in the world—so don't let me down and [send] some snapshots along also. Bye, bye, sweetheart, I love you and kiss all the boys for me and many, many for you.
As ever,
Tom

On the evening of February 23, 1944, when Captain Moore relieved his roommate, Captain Drinnen, as medical officer on duty, Drinnen said that, because of the long hours he had been working, he was very tired. He said he was going to bathe and go to bed.

A few hours later, the homeowners noticed water coming from their ceiling. They rushed upstairs to the bathroom and found Drinnen unconscious in the overflowing bathtub. The distraught British couple called for help, but every effort to resuscitate him by civilian and U.S. Army doctors were unsuccessful.

In English homes, the water for baths was heated by gas in a device called a geyser. Captain Drinnen had died as a result of poisoning from carbon monoxide that leaked from the primitive gas water heater. An investigation found that strong winds had blown gas back into the exhaust duct, which allowed the gas to build up around Drinnen while he was in the bathtub.

Captain Drinnen's army friends knew that Chaplain Frazier, who was stationed nearby, was his brother-in-law, and they summoned Frazier to come to Swindon. On February 28, 1944, Chaplain Frazier conducted a funeral, and Captain Drinnen was buried at Brookwood Cemetery, which was set aside for American soldiers. In the meantime, Frazier did his best to console Fern and to give her a description of the English cemetery where Tom was buried.

March 1, 1944
Dear Fern and Boys:
Fern, I don't know how to write this letter and what to say in it, as words are so void at times like you are going through right now. They called me to come to Tom's unit as soon as I could....I helped with the arrangements for the funeral service which was held at the limit. We tried to do things the way we thought you would want them done....I am sending you a picture of the chapel and you can see some of the beautiful evergreens....Give my love to the boys, and I pray for grace to comfort you and them. Your boys will always have a goal to strive for to be as good a man as Tom was a man and father.
Love to you all,
Cecil

A heartbroken Fern essentially merely existed for the next three months. Her depression was so great that she mostly stayed in bed and stopped eating. She packed all of Tom's letters in a box and refused to talk about him for the rest of her life. In 1948, Captain Drinnen was brought home, and Chaplain Frazier conducted a second funeral for him in Knoxville.

Slowly, Fern gained strength, which largely came from the realization that she was now going to have to be mother and father for the boys. The challenge to somehow give the boys the needed guidance, love and discipline they required and deserved steeled her resolve.

All three boys were good athletes, and she gave them opportunities to pursue these activities—that is, as long as their homework and grades did not suffer. Fern intended for her and Tom's boys to get good educations and become outstanding men. To say that Fern answered the challenge and succeeded beyond any reasonable expectations would be a gross understatement. This is exemplified by the following biographies of her three "rascals:"

Gary, the oldest son, graduated from Carson-Newman College and later received his doctorate in education (EdD) from Duke University in Durham, North Carolina. He served as principal at one elementary school and two high schools. At his retirement, the fieldhouse at Central Cabarrus County High School was named in his honor.

Thomas Jr. graduated from the University of Tennessee in Knoxville and from the University of Tennessee School of Medicine in Memphis. For over thirty years, Tommy's practice consisted largely in caring for the underserved at the University of Tennessee's Ambulatory Care Center and serving as Medical Director for Knox County's Elderly Care Hospital. During this time, he and his family did missionary work in the western African country of Liberia.

Dan graduated from Carson-Newman College and the University of Tennessee School of Medicine in Memphis. He practiced medicine as a family physician in Dickson, Tennessee, for over thirty years. He has led several medical missions to Caribbean countries in conjunction with his church's mission program. His son, Daniel Jr., also graduated from the University of Tennessee School of Medicine and is a practicing surgeon in Morristown, Tennessee, a fourth-generation Drinnen physician.

Not surprisingly, the sons who Fern single-handedly disciplined, nurtured, loved and encouraged earned doctoral degrees and went on to become highly respected members of their communities. After all, this is what Captain Thomas Drinnen would have wanted.

8

THE TRAIL OF TEARS
BEGINS IN EAST TENNESSEE

When Thomas Jefferson was president (1801–09), almost all Americans lived within fifty miles of the Atlantic Ocean. When he completed the Louisiana Purchase (820,000 square miles bought from the French for $15 million) and then commissioned the Lewis and Clark Expedition to explore the vast uncharted land all the way to the Pacific Ocean, he clearly thought America's future lay in western expansion.

Jefferson saw the American Indians and their large expanse of land to be in the way of migrating White settlers. He believed that the Indians, especially the large tribes in the Southeast, should be removed from their lands and relocated to the West. He was the first major public figure to state this belief, but he was not the last.

The bitter conflicts between White settlers and Native Americans continued almost nonstop for over two hundred years. Because the Indians were poorly armed against the settlers and often faced the U.S. Army, they lost most engagements. They were also poorly represented in court cases and generally lost there, too.

As the frontier slowly crept westward, the amount of land claimed by the American Indians in the Southeast became smaller with each passing year. As the number of settlers' farms grew rapidly, the land being hunted for food by the Indians shrank by a corresponding amount. The number of deer, the food staple for the natives, fell precipitously, causing Indian tribes to fight each other for the remaining land.

Above: Outward slanting walls of British Fort Loudoun near the Cherokee capital. *William and Marjorie Waldrop*.

Opposite, top: View of the interior of Fort Loudoun. *William and Marjorie Waldrop*.

Opposite, bottom: Storage house inside Fort Loudoun. *William and Marjorie Waldrop*.

Recognizing that the crisis was rapidly getting worse, in the early 1800s, Congress began inviting representatives selected by the Indians to come to Washington, D.C., to discuss a solution. Often wearing their culture's clothing, these representatives were a colorful spectacle as they walked the streets of the nation's capital. The Indian delegates were usually put up in the nicest available hotels. They were provided with the best food and plenty of drink. For some of the delegates, people back home in their faraway villages were often forgotten.

The Choctaws in Mississippi, losing much of their hunting lands, sent a delegation of their top chiefs to Washington. En route, one of the delegates, Apuckshunubbee, fell from a hotel balcony and broke his neck. Another delegate, Pushmataha, developed a respiratory infection that at the time was called "the croup." Without medicine to fight the infection, he knew he was dying. While on his deathbed, he was visited by Andrew Jackson, who would

become president within five years. He was also visited by John Calhoun, the secretary of war. Thinking of his brothers back home, Pushmataha told Calhoun: "I can say and tell the truth that no Choctaw ever drew his bow against the United States. My nation has given of its country until it is very small. We are in trouble."

John Quincy Adams became the country's sixth president in 1825 and immediately faced a major problem that was brewing between the Cherokees and Creeks in Georgia. He dispatched negotiators and a sizable number of troops to attempt to keep peace and see if a mutually acceptable solution could be negotiated.

The government proposed a treaty that would give the Creeks free land in Oklahoma and a yearly stipend for each affected Indian. John Ridge, a member of the Cherokees who had been schooled in Cornwall, Connecticut, wrote a reply for the Cherokees. The Creeks had no one who was literate in English, so they hired Ridge to be their negotiator and spokesman. On behalf of the Creeks, Ridge prepared a response to the government's proposal to General Edmund Gaines, the President's personal emissary. General Gaines forwarded the following message to President Adams:

Sign in front of Cherokee chief Sequoyah's Birthplace Museum. *Author's collection.*

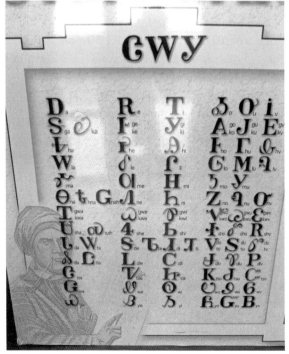

Above: Entrance to the Chief Sequoyah Birthplace Museum. *William and Marjorie Waldrop.*

Left: Cherokee alphabet as developed by Chief Sequoyah. *William and Marjorie Waldrop.*

They protest against the treaty—they refuse to receive any part of the consideration money, or to give any other evidence of their acquiescence in the Treaty. But they have in the strongest terms deliberately declared that they will not raise an arm against the United States, even should an army come to take from them the whole of their country—that they will make no sort of resistance, but will sit down quietly and be put to death, where the bones of their ancestors are deposited; that the world shall know the Muscogee nation so loved their country that they were willing to die in it rather than sell it or leave it.

Another faction of the Creeks was willing to sell only their land east of the Chattahoochee River. Their reply to General Gaines's overture was also one of nonviolence, a concept totally new to Gaines.

Further concessions cannot be made and after the reasons first assigned, more you cannot demand we now appeal to the magnanimity of the United States. We have travelled a long road to perform this duty. It is ordained by the Great Creator that we are so reduced as to be dependent on your power and mercy: and if in the hugeness of strength you determine to decide by power and not by right, we shall return to our friends and live there, until you take possession of our country. Then shall we beg bread from the whites and live the life of vagabonds on the soil of our progenitor. We shall not touch a cent of money for our lands thus forced from our hands, and not a drop of white man's blood will be spilled. And as fast as we are knocked in the head—the throats of our wives and children are cut, by the first tide of population that know not law, we will then afford the United States a spectacle of emigration, which we hope may be to a country prepared by the Great Spirit for honest and unfortunate Indians.

In a council meeting in the Cherokee capital of New Echota in July 1827, a constitution that resembled that of the United States was written. They had formed a new and separate country called the Cherokee Nation, which made things even more complicated.

According to the latest census, the Cherokee Nation owned 7,600 horses, 22,000 cows, 2,500 sheep, 2,900 plows, 2,488 spinning wheels, 18 schools, 31 gristmills, 18 ferries and 60 blacksmith shops. They maintained a large network of roads that could be used year-round.

By 1829, the situation along the frontier had grown worse. A few settlers were still being killed, but the situation for the Indians had become desperate.

Typical Cherokee home at the start of the Trail of Tears. *William and Marjorie Waldrop.*

Typical Cherokee barn. *William and Marjorie Waldrop.*

That same year, Andrew Jackson became the seventh president, and he faced the problem that his immediate predecessors had been unable to solve.

Jackson knew and liked John Ridge and sought his council. The following letter to Jackson illustrates this friendship and indicates that Ridge seems to have been warming to the government's side, even though he negotiated and spoke for the Indians: "My heart is glad when I look upon you. Our heads have become white. They are blossomed with age....We ought to thank the Great Spirit who has taken care of our lives. When first we met we were taking the red path. We waded in blood until the murders of our women and children had ceased....War is no more heard in our land. The mountains speak peace. Joy is in our valleys. The warrior...smokes the pipe of peace. His arms lay idle...he speaks to his children of his valiant deeds."

In his very first message to Congress, however, Jackson endorsed the removal of Indians from the eastern United States. This removal involved the Choctaws, Seminoles, Chickasaws, Creeks and Cherokees. Because the Cherokees were the largest of the tribes, Jackson mentioned them in particular when he told Congress that they should be moved, "voluntarily, for it would be cruel and unjust to compel them to abandon the graves of their fathers and seed a home in a distant land." He was agreeing with the sentiment that President Jefferson had articulated thirty years prior.

In its May 29, 1930 edition, the Cherokee Nation's newspaper the *Phoenix* reported: "A certain Cherokee farmer was asked by whites to sell them his horses, and he refused. They turned his horses out of the corral. While the farmer chased after his animals, white men entered his house and beat his wife unconscious. Here is the secret. Full license to our oppressors, and every avenue of justice closed to us. Yes, this is the bitter cup prepared for us...we shall drink it to the very dregs."

That same month, the Choctaws conceded and agreed to sell their lands and be relocated to the West. President Jackson personally negotiated this arrangement.

In 1831, the various Indian tribes hired lawyers William Wirt and John Sergeant to represent them in a pending case before the U.S. Supreme Court. Their opening statement summarizes their argument on behalf of the Indians.

We know that whatever can be properly done for this unfortunate people will be done by this honorable court....They have been true and faithful to us and have a right to expect a corresponding fidelity on our part. Through a long course of years they have followed our counsel with the docility of children. Our wish has been their law. We asked them to become civilized, and they became so. They assumed our dress, copied our names, pursued our course of education.…They have watched the progress of our prosperity with the strongest interest, and have marked the rising grandeur of our nation with as much pride as if they belonged to us.

On July 18, 1831, the Supreme Court ruled that the Indians could not hold the power of a foreign nation. With Congress and the Supreme Court ruling against them, the Indians' plight became more desperate.

In February 1832, a few hundred Choctaws voluntarily boarded ships on the Mississippi River to begin their trek to the West. Their leader, Chief Harkins, addressed the crowd that had gathered to see them off and made it quite clear that leaving was about the only choice remaining to them. Speaking from onboard a ship, he told the somber crowd, "to remain would be inevitable annihilation."

On April 16, the Jackson administration made a comprehensive proposal to the Indian leaders. Under this arrangement, Cherokees were offered fertile land west of the Arkansas Territory. They could travel westward in the mode of travel that they chose. They would receive a subsistence allowance for the first year. Each adult male would receive a rifle. Orphans would receive financial assistance, any livestock left behind would be paid for and White people would not be allowed in their land.

In 1834, the Cherokees argued fiercely whether they should relocate or not. During a meeting at Red Clay, Tennessee, fights broke out between the two factions, and several shots were fired. The Cherokee Nation was bankrupt, and Chief John Ridge said, "Our nation is crumbling into ruin."

President Jackson wrote a letter to the Cherokees attempting to convince them that removal to another land was in their best interest:

The choice is now before you. May the Great Spirit teach you how to choose.…Every year will increase your difficulties. Shut your ears to bad counsels. Look at your condition as it now is, and consider what it will be if you follow the advice I give you.
Your friend, Andrew Jackson—Washington, March 16, 1835

By the fall of 1836, President Jackson had grown tired of more than seven years of endless negotiations with the Indians. He reminded them that the previously agreed-to treaty, which had been signed by only a few Indians, stipulated that, two years after the Senate ratified the treaty, they had two years to move to their new homes. If they moved voluntarily before that time, they could move on their own and by any mode they chose. After that, they would be taken there under military command. He reminded them that their venerable chief Sequoyah, along with his family, were already in the territory west of the Arkansas Territory, and he reportedly liked it there.

In 1837, Martin Van Buren became the eighth president of the United States and inherited the nagging Indian removal problem. In a letter dated December 28, 1837, members of the Indian Commission in Washington, D.C., with the approval of Van Buren, wrote to the Cherokees:

> *Our official relations to the Cherokee people imposes it upon us, as a duty, to make you acquainted with the true state of your affairs.... We have long since been convinced that many of you are laboring under a dangerous error, and that you have been duped and deluded by those in whom you have placed implicit confidence. In the 16th article of the Treaty of December 29th, 1835, it is stipulated that the Cherokees "shall remove to their new homes within two years from the ratification of the treaty." —and this having occurred on the 23rd of May, 1836, you have now, after wasting opportunities, only the short period of less than five months for the settlement of your affairs here, and the preparation for your removal to your new homes.*

In the prior two or three years, over four thousand Indians had essentially given up the fight to stay in their homelands and made their own way to the new land west of the Arkansas Territory. The majority, many in denial, remained in their villages. Some planted fields of corn. The time allotted them in the treaty, however, was now gone.

In May 1838, President Van Buren appointed General Winfield Scott to round up the noncomplying Indians in the states of Tennessee, Alabama, Georgia and North Carolina. Scott assembled seven thousand soldiers consisting of infantry, cavalry and artillery units. About fifteen thousand Cherokees were located and directed to three locations along the Tennessee River. Scott instructed his officers to find places where drinking water and shade were plentiful. Some Indians, he instructed, would be sent by boat, while others would travel overland. Scott's stern message to the Cherokees made clear his intentions:

> *Cherokees! The President of the United States has sent me, with a powerful army, to cause you, in obedience to the Treaty of 1835, to join that part of your people who are already established in prosperity, on the other side of the*

Mississippi....The full moon of May is already on the wane, and before another shall have passed away, every Cherokee man, woman, and child... must be in motion to join their brethren in the far West.

Chiefs, head-men, warriors! Will you by resistance, compel us to resort to arms? God forbid! Or will you by flight, seek to hide yourselves in mountains and forests, and thus oblige us to hunt you down...spare me, I beseech you, the horror of witnessing the destruction of the Cherokees.

Realizing the sensitive nature of his assignment, Scott constantly sent messages to his troops as to how to handle their awkward task. His concern that an Indian uprising could flare up at any time was obvious in some of his instructions. He told his officers that if an Indian was too sick to be removed, a member of their family should be left with them. All strong men, women and children were to march with their military escorts. For the feeble, Indian horses and ponies would be furnished. If needed, wagons must be supplied.

The largest encampment of Cherokees was at Calhoun, Tennessee, beside the Hiwassee River. On June 6, 1838, army wagons brought approximately one thousand Indians to Ross's Landing, where they boarded one steamboat and six flatboats. They would follow the Hiwassee, Tennessee, Ohio, Mississippi and Arkansas Rivers.

Three days later, near Decatur, Tennessee, water in the Tennessee River was too low to support river traffic, so the officer in charge of the detachment, Lieutenant Edward Deas, left the encampment to arrange transportation by rail. When he returned, nearly all of the Indians were drunk and over three hundred had abandoned the boats to begin walking back to their homes.

Deas could only estimate the number of Cherokees that were still on the boats, because the Indians refused to answer a roll call. His job was made almost impossible because the remaining passengers were totally uncooperative and would not even give their names to the soldiers. Conditions were similar on the next several excursions. General Scott decided that tougher measures would need to be taken.

An excursion with eight hundred Indians left Calhoun a few days later. These Native Americans were bitter and also totally uncooperative. They refused the clothing and provisions offered them. Twenty-five Indians abandoned the ships, and several died on the journey and were buried alongside the rivers. The majority of this contingent reached Little Rock, Arkansas, and had to be put on horse-drawn wagons for the trip across the state. The weather conditions were described by the group's leader, Lieutenant Robert Whiteley.

The weather was extremely hot, a drought had prevailed for months, water was scarce, suffocating clouds of dust stirred up by oxen and wagons, and the rough rocky roads, made the sick occupants of the wagons miserable indeed. Three, four, and five deaths occurred each day....Did not move this day, the party requiring rest and being more than one-half sick; not withstanding every effort used, it was impossible to prevent their eating quantities of green peaches and corn—consequently the flux raged among them and carried off some days as high as six and seven.

By this point, things had gone so badly that General Scott agreed to allow Cherokee Chief John Ross to be in charge of taking the remaining Indians west. Ross indicated that the Indians preferred travel by land because they feared travel by boat.

When Ross returned to the forty-square-mile encampment near Calhoun, he discovered that four hundred Indians had died from multiple diseases during his time in Washington, D.C. He and General Scott agreed that the journeys west would be delayed until the cooler weather of September. More than eleven thousand Cherokees still lived east of the Mississippi River.

Ross planned to have thirteen marches with approximately nine hundred Indians in each. There would be a supply wagon pulled by four oxen for every twenty people. They would subsist mostly on salt pork and flour.

Most of the land marches used similar routes. The Tennessee River was crossed at Blythe's Ferry, which was about twelve miles from the major Calhoun encampment. The Indians traveled due west to Nashville and then north to Hopkinsville, Kentucky. They traveled northwest and crossed the Ohio and Mississippi Rivers. They traveled southwest through Missouri until they reached their new territory in what is now the state of Oklahoma.

Crossing the major rivers took several days. In addition to the Indians, hundreds of horses, mules and oxen had to be taken across. A following group sometimes had to camp a few miles from the crossing to allow the preceding party time to make the crossing. Thirteen thousand Indians and 645 wagons spanned one thousand miles of trail.

The supply wagons soon became full of sick and dying Indians. The main problem was not fatigue, but disease. Over half were now weakened by dysentery and diarrhea. The one doctor assigned to each party was in a constant state of exhaustion. They watched one of their patients die every mile.

Trail of Tears Memorial in Birchwood, Tennessee. *Author's collection.*

Trail of Tears Memorial on the waterfront in Chattanooga, Tennessee. *Author's collection.*

A traveler visited a campsite of the westward-bound Indians and reported seeing:

> *about eleven hundred Indians—sixty wagons—six hundred horses, and perhaps forty pairs of oxen. We found them in the forest camped for the night by the road side…under a severe fall of rain accompanied by heavy wind. With their canvas for a shield from the inclemency of the weather, and the cold wet ground for a resting place.…We learned from the inhabitants on the road…that they buried fourteen or fifteen at every stopping place, and they make a journey of ten miles per day only on average.*

Later, one of the more literate Indians wrote of his experience.

> *Long time we travel on way to new land. People feel bad when they leave Old Nation. Womens cry and made sad wails. Children cry and many men cry, and all look sad like when friends die, but they say nothing and just put heads down and keep on go towards West. Many days pass and people die very much.*

On March 24, 1839, two traveling parties arrived at their western destination. They had left Calhoun, Tennessee, on September 20 and October 23, 1838.

Most of the Cherokees were pleasantly surprised at how nice their new land was. There were vast fields of thick green grass, and deer and other game were abundant. It was going to be a good place for those who had survived the brutal trip west.

For some, however, old memories lingered. On June 22, 1839, John Ridge was assassinated by twenty-five of his Cherokee brethren. They could not forget their bitterness because of the treaty Ridge had negotiated that resulted in the removal from their homes in the East and had forced the proud Cherokees to walk "The Trail of Tears."

9

THE WHITE CAPS AND THE BLUE BILLS

In a courtroom in Sevierville, Tennessee, in 1892, Judge Nelson (first name unknown) said, "Gentlemen my court is hamstrung. When we bring these women in from Copeland Creek for lewdness, these men who forsake their wives and go there will just come into court and swear them out. You good citizens bring evidence against these lewd women into court each term. The grand jury returns indictments. But, when they come to trial, there's always somebody to swear them out of it."

A gentleman replied: "You're right Judge. They swear lies for these women faster than a dog trots. I ain't calling no names, but you know who I mean, in that case yesterday—he swore Hettie was the prayingest member of his church….If that woman ever started praying where I was at a meeting I'd get up and leave."

The judge continued: "Well, you see what I am up against. I can't make my court do you much good as long as these citizens keep coming in here and swearing like they do."

The frustrated judge, possibly only partly serious, said: "It looks like what you are going to have to do is form a hooded band and take bed sheets and put around you to disguise yourself and put a hood over your head so you will not be known. Then go to Copeland Creek and whip these women until they decide to straighten up and be the kind of women they should be. They are a disgrace to the community."

Another man said: "I tell you what ought to be done. What'll break it up, just get a band together and whip hell out of some of them. That'll stop it."

From this conversation, especially with the judge's input, several of the men decided that they had been given a citizen's right to form a secret organization whose members could beat "lewd" women back into respectability. The organization that was then formed became one of the most ruthless, brutal and practically unstoppable band of outlaws the United States had ever seen.

A few nights later, masked men gave severe beatings to six women who lived in Sevier County's Emert's Cove community. Within the next few days, the frightened women moved away. At first, some in the county shrugged off the attack and seemed to think, "It was a good riddance."

The secret organization, now being called the White Caps, began to recruit men from all over the county. The members would stand around the man being inducted, with their pistols cocked and held at his chest, while an oath was administered. The following oath bound them to stand by its members by keeping secret their identities and all their actions:

I do solemnly swear before God and man that if I reveal anything concerning our organization or anything we may do the penalty shall be to receive 100 lashes and leave the country within 10 days or to be put to death. Now I take this oath freely and voluntarily and am willing to abide by the obligation in every respect. I further agree and swear before God that if I reveal anything concerning our organization, I will suffer my throat to be cut, my heart to be shot out and my body to be burned: that I will forfeit my life, my property and all that I have in this world and in the world to come—so help me God.

The new member understood that if a member violated his oath by identifying any of the members or making known any of the group's secrets, two members would be selected randomly to put the "traitor" to death. After taking the oath, the new member was given the right hand of fellowship and told he was a full-fledged member.

The White Caps adopted a secret signal to identify another member. Passing the right hand over the right cheek indicated, "I'm a White Cap." Passing the left hand over the left cheek answered, "So am I."

From the start, the White Caps wore masks with small holes cut for their eyes, nose and mouth. They wore loose white gowns on their night missions to whip their unfortunate targets.

Within a few months of organizing, the White Caps had developed a new strategy to help their members who testified in court. They privately changed their name to "Grave Yard Hosts." With this change, when a member was asked if he was a member of the White Caps or if he had ever been on a White Cap raid, he could answer truthfully, at least in his own mind, in the negative.

The secret organization soon branched out from its original reason for being and started attacking men as well. The members had become vigilantes and felt they had the right to enforce the law as they saw fit. Ominously, they quickly became numerous enough so that every jury that was seated had at least one member in it. When a White Cap member came to trial, he was always exonerated. This organization had its own physicians, who would often treat wounded members of the White Caps, and no one in the community knew about the injury.

Because the law in Sevier County was impotent against the White Cap terrorists, other citizens formed a group similar to vigilantes. The Blue Bills were organized for the sole purpose of stopping the ruthless White Caps. While the White Caps had about one thousand members on its rolls, the most that the Blue Bills ever had was about two hundred. Because the Blue Bills were better armed and consisted of men who were more dedicated to their mission, the strength of the two sides was fairly equal.

On a cold November night in 1894 near Henderson Springs, a battle between the White Caps and the Blue Bills occurred. The White Caps were routed and sent home. The next morning, the bodies of Elijah Helton, a member of the Blue Bills, and Laban Latham and Isaac Keeble, of the White Caps, were found.

Earlier in the evening, the White Caps had knocked down the door of James and Ruth Massey and took them outside and gave them a severe beating. They beat Ruth so severely over her entire body that she passed out. The Blue Bills encountered the White Caps as they were on their way home after the beatings.

The people who saw the Masseys' injuries were sickened and wanted very badly to find a way to avenge these beatings. Nine members of the White Caps were arrested for the beatings. Because two other members of the secret organization were on the grand jury, no true bill was found. The jury was always stacked in favor of the White Caps, because their lawyer would give the secret signal to a prospective juror, and if it was answered by the proper signal, the juror was seated. If the signal was not returned to the lawyer, the person was dismissed.

The White Caps often came to court with their own suborned witnesses. Witnesses for the state were often threatened, and several people left the state to avoid testifying against the White Caps.

Laura Rose and her two small children lived in the Nunn's Cove area of Sevier County. One morning, she opened her front door and found two hickory switches and a note that read, "Laura Rose, You get out of this house in five days or we'll give you 75 licks." It was signed, "Sevier County White Caps."

Laura grabbed her children and ran to the home of Tom Walker, a known Blue Bill. Walker took her to a house twelve miles away only to find a note that read, "You cannot live in this house either." It was well after midnight when they made it back to Tom Walker's house. He then took them to Campbell Dugan's house, where they were safe for the rest of the night.

The next morning, Walker moved Laura and her children to his house, where he found a note warning him not to move Laura Rose another time. At this, Walker was enraged and started swearing loudly. He immediately went into Sevierville and bought several sticks of dynamite and additional ammunition for his guns and said if the White Caps ever came after him they would have a hot welcome.

After being moved two more times, Laura Rose decided to return home because she knew no other place to go. She was still uneasy and would sometimes go to a friendly neighbor and stay the night. While at the home of Frank Keeler one night, ten men knocked down the Keelers' front door and dragged Laura outside and began to beat her unmercifully. One man held her while another one beat her with a lash. With the woman unconscious, the men mounted their horses and rode off into the night.

As promised, when the White Caps came after Tom Walker, he was ready for them. Three came up and knocked on his front door while several waited in the yard. When the trio started kicking in the door, Walker, who was hiding under a bridge only a few yards from the raiders, touched a wire to a battery that set off a tremendous dynamite explosion. Men and horses littered the front yard. Every time one of the outlaws moved, Walker shot him with his Winchester shotgun. The number of dead and wounded was never known.

Several decent men had joined the White Caps, because they initially thought its goal was good for their community. Some soon learned that they had actually joined a lawless band and were constantly reminded of their oath and that to attempt to leave meant their death. A high percentage did, however, become largely inactive, leaving mainly thugs to run the organization. The White Caps sank deeper into crime against the general population and were now murdering and robbing with greater frequency.

They often chose elderly people, who likely had their savings hidden on their premises. Generally, five or six White Caps would break in and rob the defenseless at gunpoint, often taking their life savings.

The territory controlled by the White Caps became a place of refuge for anyone who had committed a crime of any sort and was on the run from the law. Strangers were taken in and treated as if they were part of the organization. They were given access to the White Caps' crooked lawyers, "expert witnesses" and sham juries. They were guaranteed of an acquittal.

William and Laura Whaley were a young couple with a six-week-old baby named Molly Lillard. Somehow, Laura found out some of the White Cap secrets and told a friend about it. When the White Caps learned of this, she was told she must die. At night, two men broke into their house and executed Laura and William. Laura's older sister, Lizzie Chandler, and the Whaleys' baby were in the corner of the room in bed. Lizzie was only a few feet away from the murderers and could see their faces clearly.

Infuriated citizens came from miles around to view the bodies of the young couple. They were so upset at the sight that they decided enough was enough; they would no longer tolerate the evil organization that had terrorized their county for more than three years. They would do whatever it took to rid the county of the ruthless outlaws.

In his book *The White Caps of Sevier County*, Sevier County resident Cas Walker wrote of the irate people at the murder scene.

It was too much for the people to bear. It was beyond toleration. They broke forth, as it were, in their fury, and were aroused as men seldom are. Every good citizen swore in his heart to assist in avenging the murder of the Whaleys and putting an end to the infamous White Cap practices. When the five hundred people…viewed the remains of William and Laura Whaley as they lay prostrate upon the floor of their cabin home in their night apparel and in pools of blood, and heard the piteous cries of the little babe that in so short a time had been rendered parentless and homeless, the smoldering fires that had slumbered in their breasts so long now broke forth like volcanoes and with such fury that it astounded the White Caps themselves. Men, who heretofore had not dared express their sentiments, now spoke them freely, and the talk became epidemic. Correct public sentiment began to reassert itself. Attorneys were employed to assist in prosecutions…all suspicious persons, especially White Caps, were constantly watched.…Public sentiment was now right, and the good

*and law abiding people were determined to beat no retreat....It was felt
that something must be done to exclude White Caps from sitting on juries,
both grand and petit, for as long as they were on the juries there was but
little hope of successful prosecutions.*

It took investigators several weeks to discover that Bob Catlett, the
clandestine leader of the White Caps, had paid $125 to Pleas Wynn and
$125 to Catlett Tipton to murder the Whaleys. Wynn and Tipton were
indicted for murder. Catlett and his associate, Bob Wade, were indicted as
accessories before the fact. To the surprise of all four, the trial would not be
held in Sevier County but in a totally different venue. Their trial would be in
Morristown, Tennessee, in the county of Hamblen. The first trial would be
for the murder of Laura Whaley.

In November 1897, it took five days for the lawyers and judge to select
12 jurors from the 1,200 who had been subpoenaed. It was difficult to find
jurors who had not already formed an opinion in the case.

Defense lawyers were quick to attempt to impeach the character of Lizzie
Chandler, the only eyewitness to the murder. They brought up her former
husband's derogatory testimony at their divorce proceedings, but Lizzie was
not fazed by the attacks and calmly told her story. To most observers, her
story was one of truthfulness.

When Lizzie was asked to point out the man who did the shooting, she
looked around the quiet courtroom. She glanced from one face to another
until she spotted the face of Pleas Wynn. She then looked up at the judge.
He asked, "Have you found him?"

"Yes," she answered.

The district attorney asked, "Where is he?"

"There," she said and pointed at Wynn. She added, "He is the man who
had the gun on the night of the murder."

The next day, the jury returned a guilty verdict against Pleas Wynn but
acquitted Catlett Tipton. Both men would still stand trial for the murder of
William Whaley. Wynn was taken to jail in Knoxville to await the next trial.
Tipton was held on a bond of $10,000.

In March 1898, Pleas Wynn and Catlett Tipton were tried for the murder
of William Whaley. As in the Laura Whaley case, twelve hundred prospective
jurors were questioned before a jury could be seated. The case was submitted
to the jury in the afternoon of April 8. The following day, the jury returned
a verdict of guilty in the first degree. The two men were sentenced to be
hanged on January 4, 1899.

Bob Catlett, the man who allegedly paid Wynn and Tipton for the murder of the Whaleys and was charged as an accessory, was next to go on trial. His counsel requested a change of venue because they knew that everyone in Sevier County suspected that Catlett was the ringleader of the White Caps. They argued that he could not get a fair trial. The request was granted, and the venue was changed to Morristown in Hamblen County, similar to the trial of Wynn and Tipton.

In the meantime, Wynn and Tipton agreed to confess to their crimes in order to implicate the man who they said paid them. The governor of Tennessee ordered the delay of their execution for two months so their confessions could be heard at Bob Catlett's trial. Part of Pleas Wynn's confession follows.

> *Catlett took me back into the stable in a side room, and there mentioned to me the first time about putting the Whaleys out of the way. He asked me if I had had a talk with Catlett Tipton lately, and if I had agreed to go to a certain place with him. I told him that I had talked with him and had agreed to go. He told me he had agreed to pay Tipton $50.00 to kill the Whaleys, pay his lawyer's fees and keep him out of jail if anything should be found out on him…he wanted it done that night, while he was away, so he would not be suspected and could prove where he was.*

Catlett Tipton's testimony in the trial of Bob Catlett included the following:

> *It was not long, however, until Catlett returned to me again and began to beg me to comply with his wishes by putting the Whaleys out of the way. I guess in all, he must have come to me some twelve or fifteen different times, and I at last consented to kill the Whaleys for him, for which he agreed to pay me fifty dollars, and if I got into any trouble over it, he was to pay my attorney's fees and keep me out of jail by making bond for me.…I told Catlett I had spoken to Pleas Wynn to go with me and that he had agreed to go. He asked me if I thought Pleas would be all right and I told him I did.*

Testifying on behalf of his brother at the trial, Jim Catlett admitted to being in Sevierville the day after the Whaleys were killed but denied that he had paid fifty dollars to the killers. He said that he did not have anywhere near that much money on that day.

Sign at the cemetery where Pleas Wynn was buried. *Author's collection.*

The state then introduced A.T. Marshall, assistant cashier of the Bank of Sevierville. He testified that on the day in question, December 29, he paid fifty dollars to Jim Catlett. He presented the bank books to prove it. The state promptly closed its case.

The case went to the jury on a Friday evening. By Saturday morning, an unknown disagreement among the jurors was so violent that the judge dismissed the jurors and declared a mistrial. Over the next several months, Bob Catlett's case was continued from one court to another until the charge wore itself out. The case was dropped, and Catlett was a free man.

Pleas Wynn and Catlett Tipton were not as fortunate. The following eyewitness article written by *Knoxville Weekly Sentinel* reporter W.P. Chandler describes the double hanging.

> *Sevierville, July 5—Pleas Wynn and Catlett Tipton shot through the death trap on the gallows here at 1:05 p.m. today. They were dead a few minutes thereafter. The march to the scaffold was begun a few minutes before 1:00.... The death warrants were read just before leaving the jail.... The men displayed remarkable nerve to the end...about the scaffold in*

Left: Tombstone of Pleas Wynn. *Right*: Tombstone of Catlett Tipton. *Author's collection.*

> the enclosure were 96 people. Many of these were relatives of Wynn and
> Tipton....The little company on the scaffold sang, "I Need Thee Every
> Hour." The two heart-broken wives were led from the scaffold....At exactly
> 1:02, Deputy Keener pulled the trap.

The tragic deaths of William and Laura Whaley were avenged by the execution of their killers and also by the death of the once-feared organization called the White Caps.

10

A TROUBLED YOUNG MAN IS GIVEN MORE THAN A SECOND CHANCE

November 8, 2005, began routinely for Kenneth Bartley, but conditions would change dramatically after he found his father's .22-caliber handgun in their home. With the weapon in his pocket, he first thought to trade it to a neighbor for some OxyContin. He did not do this, however, and his subsequent actions led him to describe the day as "the worst day of many people's lives."

At his high school in Jacksboro, Tennessee, Bartley showed the weapon to some of his fellow students, who quickly alerted school authorities. He was immediately summoned to the principal's office, where principal Gary Seale and assistant principals Ken Bruce and Jim Pierce were waiting.

Seale asked Bartley to remove the weapon from his pocket. When he did, Seale asked, "Kenny, is that thing real?"

Bartley replied: "I'll show you it's real. I never liked you anyway."

Bartley loaded a clip in the gun and fired two or three shots at Seale. He then turned to Bruce, who had his arms in the air. Bruce was shot, and he slid down to the floor with his back against a filing cabinet. Pierce wrestled Bartley to the floor but was shot in the process. In approximately three seconds, six shots were fired. Assistant principal Ken Bruce was taken by ambulance to St. Mary's Hospital, about five miles away in Lafollette, Tennessee, where he died a few minutes later. Seriously wounded, Seale and Pierce were airlifted to the University of Tennessee Hospital. Both survived.

Bartley, who had suffered a shot to his hand, was also taken to the hospital in Lafollette. When treated and released, he was seen wearing a yellow blood-spattered shirt and getting into a sheriff's car.

When interviewed by reporters a few days later, Seale was puzzled as to how he had survived. He said, "There's no way somebody aims a gun at your head and misses killing you at that range." Student Nathan Lawson said that the murdered assistant principal Ken Bruce had always lent a willing ear to the students. "He was a nice guy. If you went to talk to him about any problems you had, he'd be a person who would listen."

A few days after the shooting, Bartley was interviewed by a psychologist, who learned that the young man's father was an alcoholic and his parents had divorced a couple of years prior. The psychologist said: "The parents' neglect was profound, and the young man was basically on his own to survive in an unsafe environment. A child in this situation becomes neurologically hard-wired to do whatever it takes to survive."

In 2007, it was time for Bartley to face trial for first-degree murder. Because his crime had been so heinous, he was to be tried as an adult.

A few days before the trial began, Bartley's lawyers announced a plea deal in which Bartley agreed to a term of forty-five years in prison. His lawyers later moved to withdraw the arrangement. The court was told that the accused had not had time to consult with his parents and the details had never been read to him in full. Everyone familiar with the case was stunned when the judge set aside the agreement and granted Bartley a new trial, which was scheduled for 2014. At this point, Bartley had served eight years of his forty-five-year sentence.

At this trial, Bartley took the witness stand and testified calmly. Several times, he apologized for his actions. Also, he told the jury that he had loaded the gun at home and not at school. He denied ever making the statement about never liking Seale.

He stated that just before being called to the principal's office he had crushed and snorted Xanax. It was his belief that his actions were attributable to his being high and scared. "As I cocked the gun, I saw Mr. Pierce swivel in his chair....I thought he was coming at me. That's when I fired the first shot....I honestly can't recall the exact sequence of the shots after that."

Everyone in the packed courtroom sat in stunned silence when the verdict was read. The jury acquitted Bartley of first-degree murder but found him guilty of the lesser charge of reckless homicide. Instead of forty-five years behind bars, Bartley walked out of the courtroom a free man. He had already served enough time to fulfill the sentence for the lesser crime. Several people in the courtroom sat and sobbed. Nearly all called it a miscarriage of justice.

A few days later, Bartley said in an interview that he was "not going to waste another chance. All I want is to be able to go out here and be

IN GOD WE TRUST

Campbell County Courthouse, the site of Kenneth Bartley's trials. *Author's collection.*

somebody more than the Campbell County school shooter. I'm trying to make this work. I am going to make this work."

Bartley's conversion did not last long, however. He quickly found himself in trouble with the law when he was charged with threatening to kill his father because of an argument about a set of car keys. Then he was arrested because of a violent argument with his mother over a seventy-dollar cab fare.

Just as Bartley's life was nearing another low point, he got help from an unlikely source. At the time of his 2007 trial, Erin Tepaske, who was getting her master's degree in counseling, offered to help Bartley turn his life around. She said that she was drawn to these difficult cases and that this case spurred her to begin working as an activist on juvenile justice issues.

Tepaske said, "He did a horrible thing, but I also saw the other side of it—how horribly it was handled." She was mainly referring to the fact that Bartley was being tried as an adult.

Tepaske drew up a plan detailing how she would offer counseling as she got Bartley off drugs and help him find a job. She offered that Bartley could stay in her home in Virginia. Judge E. Shayne Sexton thought the arrangement was unusual, but he approved the plan anyway. He later said, "Frankly, it looked very good on paper."

So, with the concurrence of the court, Bartley was off to live with his counselor in Virginia. Tepaske reported later that things went well initially as Bartley got used to having her three-year-old son, Beckett Josef Podominick, around all the time. She said that Bartley seemed to thrive in his new surroundings and seemed to have a positive influence on her son.

Tepaske said that she taught Bartley how to cook and how to navigate on street buses. She also instructed him how to dress professionally for the times he would go on job interviews.

On Mother's Day in 2015, the relationship between Tepaske and Bartley experienced a sudden and heartbreaking turn. That afternoon, the mother decided to explore a nearby park on her own and left Bartley to look after her little son.

At one point, Bartley texted Tepaske that everything was going well. A short time later, Bartley called Tepaske to tell her that Beckett had fallen and was not acting right. She instructed Bartley to call 911 and she rushed home. She would later say, "Knowing that ambulance was coming to get my Baby was the worst nightmare."

At Inova Fairfax Hospital, doctors discovered a long fracture from the back of Beckett's skull to the top. The boy's brain had severe swelling, and the doctors believed that he had little chance of survival.

Tepaske noticed that there were few outward signs of injury and Beckett looked like he was asleep. On May 12, Tepaske's former husband was present at the hospital when they decided to remove life support from their son, who immediately died.

After Beckett's death, Tepaske said she asked Bartley many times to describe what had happened in her backyard when her son had been mortally injured. She knew very well that because of Bartley's history, this case would be closely scrutinized.

Bartley told the same story over and over to Tepaske. He told her that he and Beckett were playing in the backyard when Beckett ran up the three steps that led to the back door and began pulling hard on the door. When Beckett's grip slipped, he fell backward and hit the back of his head on some concrete pavers and rocks. Bartley said that he was almost close enough to catch the boy but only managed to grab his shirt. Tepaske said that after going over the incident many times with Bartley, she believed him completely.

The Medical Director of the Forensic Assessment Department of Inova Fairfax Hospital, William Houda, examined Beckett when he was still alive.

He was asked to examine six wounds on the back of Beckett's head that did not appear to have been caused by the fall that Bartley described.

Houda described the injuries as coming from an object with two prongs, but he was not sure what this object could have been. He said, "That troubled me." After carefully examining Beckett's body, Hauda concluded that the type of fall Bartley described "does not commonly cause such a severe injury." A study by the American Association of Pediatrics estimated the annual mortality rate for toddlers suffering short falls to be less than one in one million.

In July 2015, the Virginia Medical Examiner ruled that Beckett had died of blunt-force head trauma. He said that there was not enough available evidence to determine if the boy's death had been accidental or a homicide, so the death was recorded as "undetermined."

The following October, the Fairfax County Child Protective Services concluded its investigation into Beckett's death and reported a startling discovery. They were certain that, prior to his death, the boy had been abused.

The boy's father, Matthew Podominick, could not believe what he was hearing. He said: "I collapsed on the floor. I wept. I was so sad, furious, beyond angry, mad, confused, and devastated." Podominick wrote to the governors of Tennessee and Virginia accusing Bartley of having a role in his son's death and asking them to start a criminal probe. He wrote, "It is now obvious to me that she put her love for Kenny Bartley over our son's safety and well-being."

Bartley had no comment for reporters. He was sent back to a jail in Tennessee to await charges of probation violations.

In March 2016, Bartley was once again arrested on a violation of probation charge. He served the balance of his probation term and was released in October.

In November 2017, Bartley was charged with trying to break into a Salvation Army office in Knoxville. He was sentenced to thirty days' probation.

On August 27, 2018, Bartley was arrested for aggravated assault when he allegedly threatened his father's girlfriend. She said he demanded money from her, and when she refused, he said: "Get out of my face. I will kill you!" She said that when she picked up a revolver and aimed it at the ground, Bartley left her home. The police picked him up. She told the police that Bartley had threatened her before and that she feared for her life.

On January 28, 2019, when Bartley's trial for assaulting his father's girlfriend was about to begin, his lawyer, Wesley Brooks, asked the judge to move the trial to another county. He described the news media as "often

Ken Bruce Memorial Highway sign. *Author's collection.*

excessive, hostile, and inflammatory. Many in the community feel as though Bartley was not punished appropriately in the school shooting" and that Bartley could not receive a fair trial in Campbell County.

Judge E. Shayne Sexton did not allow a change of venue, and Bartley once again went on trial in Campbell County. It took the jury forty-five minutes to acquit him. Judge Sexton said, "Mr. Bartley you are free to go." At the time of the trial, Bartley was living in the LaFollette, Tennessee area. The "Ken Bruce Memorial" highway runs through the center of the city.

11

"THUNDER WAS HIS ENGINE AND WHITE LIGHTNIN' WAS HIS LOAD"

For over three thousand years, man has been making intoxicating drink, which he consumes himself or distributes and sells to others. Inebriating drink was mentioned by writers in the Old Testament. When many countries were losing as much as half their population during the Black Plague epidemic of the 1300s, alcoholic drink was used to ease the pain of the dying. From its extensive use at that time, it grew more popular as people used it to simply ease life's pains in general.

The word *whiskey* came from the Irish, who were the world's leaders in the manufacture of the product. In 1556, Britain, under the pretense that it was interested in saving grain for food, passed a law that imposed the death penalty on anyone caught operating a distillery. Risking death, distillers started operating under the cover of darkness. This brought about the nickname "moonshiners." Nobility was exempted from the law.

When large numbers of immigrants came to America from Ireland and Scotland, they brought their whiskey-making skills with them. Because they were constantly shadowed by law enforcement, they fled as far west as they could at that time. Large numbers settled in the mountains of North Carolina, Tennessee and Kentucky.

In some states, whiskey-making was legal when processed in state-approved facilities and bonded and labeled with a tax stamp. In fact, prior to income tax in the United States, funds from the sale of alcohol was the country's largest source of revenue.

During the Depression, jobs in the mountain areas of North Carolina, Tennessee and Kentucky were almost nonexistent. To earn money to support their often large families, many of those who owned small farms grew corn and other grains, which they distilled into alcoholic drinks. When thousands of these stills started producing a large volume of whiskey, the problem became one of getting the "splo" to their customers, who were spread over the entire southeastern United States. Getting their product to the far reaches of this vast area was made more difficult and dangerous by the seemingly constant presence of lawmen, who faced the almost hopeless task of shutting down the bootleggers' illegal operations. The network that the bootleggers had set up was much more complex and widespread than when they got their unique name by simply hiding a bottle of alcoholic beverage in their boot.

The fast cars of the whiskey runners and their ability to expertly handle them in the mountains of North Carolina played a large role in the formation of NASCAR. Writer Chris Smith points out this connection in an August 22, 2016 article in Wheelscene, a hot-rodder's website: "NASCAR'S roots are steeped in the driving skills, mechanical tricks, and just pure craziness that teenage 'shine' drivers brought to the game of cat and mouse that they played with US Treasury Department agents (known as 'revenuers')." In time, the revenuers, who were constantly chasing the haulers, contracted some of them to teach the lawmen themselves how to make a U-turn at high speed.

Roscoe "Doc" Combs, who made whiskey in Wilkes County, North Carolina, said:

The reason I started making whiskey was that there wasn't any money to be made around here. That was the only way you could make any money, so that's what I did....I got up to where I was making...800 cases a week....I had a truck that had, "Butter, Eggs, and Cheese" on the door.

In the earlier days, we could find out what roads to stay off of, which ones not to be on, on certain days. We had a man who could go to the federal man and find out. I don't believe it cost us but $20 a week to find out all that...I made a race car for Junior Johnson and one for Hardin Benton. I fixed team cars with Cadillac motors, put three carburetors on them things, and they'd outrun the wind, just about. That was in the 1950s. They would solid fly. The law never caught one "less something" happened.

Treasury Agent Joe Carter described the federal agents' cars: "The government gave us cars that were bought on bid. I called them 'mechanical miscarriages' because they must have had sewing machine motors in them. We didn't do too good in catching the moonshiners on the road.…I don't recall an agent ever catchin' a moonshiner car to car, driving man to man."

Usually, when an agent was able to locate one of the moonshiners' hot cars, it would become his car to use in his chases. Carter said that the federal agents were totally outclassed in their driving abilities when compared to the men they were chasing. He said: "I often tell people that I'm the only federal agent to catch the great Junior Johnson, the famous race driver. When everybody looks at me in disbelief, I tell them I have to be honest and tell them that I caught him on foot, not in an automobile. There's never been an officer that could catch Junior Johnson in a car."

In the 1940s and 1950s, thousands of moonshine stills were in operation in East Tennessee. Two of the roads that were used to transport the illegal whiskey were called "Thunder Road" and "White Lightnin' Trail." These roads generally ran from northeast to southwest and from north to south, respectively. Knoxville was the unofficial hub for these roads as the heavily laden cars traveled toward the largest cities of the Deep South.

Thunder Road nominally started in the Harlan, Kentucky area and went through Middlesboro, Kentucky, and Tazewell, Maynardville and Knoxville in Tennessee.

Thunder Road

In his book *Return to Thunder Road*, Alex Gabbard wrote the following about moonshining in Tennessee:

> *Moonshine came to be what it was around here because the people were dirt poor. Even if you weren't in the Depression, you could raise crops, but you couldn't make any money doing it. They used to say that you could get fifty acres of corn on a mule's back if you distilled it.…Newport, Tennessee, was apparently the southern end of a bootlegging concern run out of Chicago. There were a lot of local people who had connections up in Chicago because the area was kind of isolated and was known as kind of a resort for its hotels. When it would get hot on those guys up there, they would gather in Hot Springs, Arkansas, Asheville, North Carolina, and Newport, Tennessee, and some other places that were good places to hide."*

Above: Intersection in West Knoxville where Robert Mitchum's character perished in the film *Thunder Road*. *Author's collection.*

Left: Moonshine still in restaurant on "Thunder Road." *Rebecca Henry.*

Glen "Mooney" Ramsey of Cosby, Tennessee, said, "There wasn't nothin' else to do but hoe corn and make moonshine. I got started when my father give me four barrels sweetened…you had to wait for the yeast to work 'em off to get 'em ready to make moonshine…a barrel would make about six gallons of white lightnin'.…We'd put the corn in the ground 'till it started sproutin', then make corn liquor.…For a fifty-gallon barrel of corn mash, it'd take a sack of bran and a hundred pounds of sugar."

Mooney continued:

If you was goin' to haul it to Knoxville, you'd cut the back end out of a '40 Ford or a '36 Ford....If you took the front seat out and put in a little seat, you could haul more....When I was makin' moonshine, there might have been maybe twenty-five stills runnin' spread around the countryside....The last load I hauled was when they was buildin' a new bridge across the river into Knoxville and they run a ferry boat across the river. We had a '36 Ford loaded with moonshine, and we had to take it across on the ferry. The 'man' jerked the door open and said, "How much you got in here tonight? Caught one just like it last night." So, we hit the water...tore a chunk out of my leg....I outrun 'em all the time. See, you had to build your own engine, shave your heads to ten thousandths, put you a set of hot heads on it, have your motor bored out. I had a '39 Ford that'd run 85 in second gear. I didn't dread anything.

The road south from Cosby never became as well known as other routes, but the amount of moonshine transported over it likely rivaled that of the more "popular" routes of "Thunder Road" and "White Lightnin' Trail."

According to writer Gabbard, Hollywood's 1957 movie *Thunder Road* was based on a real run by a real moonshine runner. Robert Mitchum, driving a car called "Whipporwill," stars in the movie that covers the approximately one hundred miles from Harlan to Knoxville. The moonshine that was destined for Memphis made it only as far as the bottom of Knoxville's Bearden hill.

The Whipporwill turned west on Knoxville's Kingston Pike and crossed over Bearden Hill. The speeding, high-powered and fully loaded car overshot the junction where Papermill Road joins Kingston Pike. The car—and the driver (Mitchum)—went down a steep bank, rolled over and crashed through a utilities substation. The car struck one of the transformers, caught fire and, with its driver, burned in an open field.

Thunder Road Ballad
Written by Robert Mitchum and Don Raye, sung by Keely Smith
Courtesy of United Artists

Oh. Let me tell the story,
I can tell it all.
About the mountain boy,

Who ran illegal alcohol.
His daddy made the whiskey,
The son, he drove the load.
And when his engine roared,
They called it Thunder Road.

Sometimes into Asheville,
Sometimes Memphis town.
The "revenooers" chased him,
But they couldn't run him down.
Each time they thought they had him,
His engine would explode.
And he'd go by like they
Were standin' still on Thunder Road.

On the 1ˢᵗ of April, 1954,
The federal man sent word.
He'd better make his run no more.
He sent two hundred agents,
Were coverin' the state.
Whichever road he tried to take,
They'd get him sure as fate.

Roarin' out of Harlan,
Revvin' up his mill.
He shot the Gap at Cumberland,
And screamed past Maynardville,
With G-men on his tail lights,
Road blocks up ahead.
The mountain boy took roads,
That angels fear to tread.

Blazing right through Knoxville,
Out on Kingston Pike.
Then right outside of Bearden,
They made the fatal strike.
He left the road at ninety,
That's all there is to say.
The devil got the moonshine,

And the mountain boy that day.
Thunder, thunder, over Thunder Road,
Thunder was his engine and
White lightnin' was his load.
Moonshine, moonshine, to quench the devil's thirst,
The law they swore they'd get him,
But the devil got him first.

The law, they never got him,
'Cause the devil got him first.

White Lightnin' Trail

White Lightnin' Trail was a few miles west of Thunder Road. The stills that supplied this route were located largely in the Appalachian Mountains of Tennessee and Kentucky. It generally followed U.S. Highway 25 and ran through LaFollette, Caryville, Lake City, Clinton and Knoxville.

In July 1933, whiskey runners shot and killed popular Anderson County sheriff Cleve Daugherty. The thirty-eight-year-old sheriff and five deputies were trying to stop three men they suspected of transporting illegal whiskey. The sheriff was hit by a blast from a 12-gauge shotgun. He died before the deputies could reach him.

Daugherty had received a tip that twenty-five half-gallon jars of whiskey were to be delivered to the Piney Woods community of Anderson County. The lawmen formed a circle around the designated place of delivery, and when three men came up the road with sacks on their shoulders, the sheriff yelled, "You're under arrest." Ignoring the order, the men started firing their weapons. When the firing stopped, one man was placed under arrest. The other two were tracked down by bloodhounds.

The *Anderson County News* reported on funeral services for the sheriff: "It was nearly 30 minutes after the hour set for the services at the First Baptist Church that the procession began to move from the county jail, three blocks distant. For nearly an hour before the time of the funeral, traffic officers kept the block in front of the church clear of heavy traffic."

In his eulogy to the slain sheriff, H.L. Smith said:

In the slaying of Cleve Daugherty, sin has played its role again. In his death we see some things that sin does even for those who are law-abiding and upright citizens. By this tragedy this county suffers, his friends suffer and his home is torn and broken. Four children are left orphans, suffering because liquor and sin took the law into its own hands. The more I see of the evils of liquor, the suffering and sorrow, the grief and disappointment that is the direct cause of this underworld tool of sin, I am made to see more clearly reasons why officers like Sheriff Daugherty are so bitterly opposed to the damnable sad life-taking stuff. To his widow, four children, father and mother and two sisters, may we say that, "Vengeance is mine, saith the Lord." God and the law will take care of the criminal. Justice will be rendered in due season.

Between 1954 and 1964, former U.S. Treasury agent Charlie Weems worked mainly in the Appalachian Mountains area. In his book *A Breed Apart*, he describes his career chasing moonshiners.

Federal law enforcement waged a war against organized whiskey production throughout the southeast and concentrated on big operations that produced 1,000 gallons of white lightnin' a day, and more. Although small-time bootleggers were also their targets, it was the big-time operators they were mostly after. Not only were they violators of multiple aspects of the law, huge quantities of whiskey generated such large sums of money that law enforcement officials were also corrupted....During this period, ATF agents in the Southeast region...seized and destroyed 72,159 stills, and 1,712,438 gallons of moonshine and arrested 71,266 violators.

The whiskey alone constituted a tax fraud on the United States of over 18 million dollars, not including taxes lost to local and state governments. Twelve ATF agents were killed in the line of duty during this same time period. Almost every agent who worked in the southeast was injured, either by direct confrontation with liquor law violators or in their pursuit....It is now part of a bygone era.

On the evening of Friday, October 29, 1943, seven-year-old Haskel "Hack" Ayers opened a gate for his father, John, and his uncle Rosco to pass through on their way to a barn that was situated about three hundred feet from Highway 25W, or White Lightnin' Trail. Hack's older sister Jerlene had called their dad at his business about 5:30 p.m. and told him that five Tennessee Highway patrolmen had come with search warrants. Several lawmen were waiting in the barn for the arrival of "High Johnny" Ayers and his brother Rosco. High Johnny called out for Hack to go to his mother.

Above: Barn where Hack Ayers's father was gunned down by police officers. *Author's collection*.

Opposite, top: Hack Ayers. *Author's collection*.

Opposite, bottom: Ayers Real Estate and Auctioneering Company. *Author's collection*.

Johnny had a 12-gauge double-barrel shotgun, and Rosco had a .45-caliber pistol. As the brothers neared the barn, they were met by a rain of bullets coming from the barn.

Hack's mother grabbed him by the hand, and they went to check on John and Rosco Ayers. When they got close to the barn, they heard one of the officers say, "I got him." They found Rosco standing, unharmed, with a gun in his hand. John was lying behind an automobile that had thirty-two bullet holes. One bullet went through John's leather jacket near his heart, and he had died almost instantly.

The lawmen had received information that John, Rosco and Hack had traveled to Middlesboro, Kentucky, that morning to pick up several cases of illegal whiskey. The Ayers brothers had made this trip several times before to get whiskey to sell in an effort to help finance the restaurant and motel that John owned.

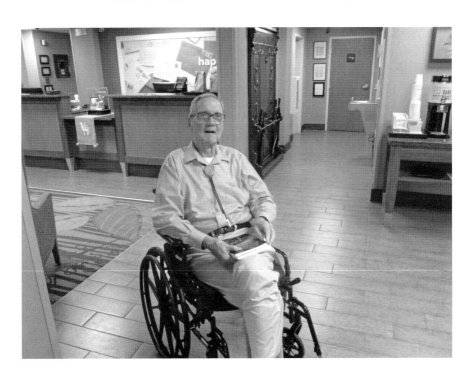

Hampton Inn owned by Hack Ayers. *Author's collection*.

View of the Cumberland Mountains from Ayers's hotel. *Author's collection*.

Jacket worn by Hack Ayers's father showing small bullet hole below zipper. *Author's collection.*

Jerlene told investigators that when the lawmen discovered the whiskey hidden in a chicken coop beside the barn, they opened a case and started drinking. The investigators were already suspicious of the way the situation had been handled by the police officers, and they put a lot of credence in Jerlene's statement. The week after the fatal shooting, arrest warrants were issued for the five officers. Chief Burdette, Sergeant Williamson and Patrolmen Purkey, Huff and Petree were charged for the murder of John Ayers, but a grand jury failed to indict them. The five were released.

Hack Ayers went on to become president of the National Auctioneer's Association and served two terms as a state representative for Campbell and Scott Counties. He became one of the most successful businessmen in Campbell County. He owns the Hampton Inn and Comfort Inn in Caryville and "Hack" Ayers Real Estate and Auctioneering Company in LaFollette. The latter company is located just in front of the barn where his father was killed.

The Sears & Roebuck leather jacket with a small bullet hole that High Johnny was wearing when he was killed hangs in the lobby of the Hampton Inn. It seems to be a way for Hack to maintain a connection with and a memory of High Johnny.

12

A WORLD'S FAIR AND A CRUMBLING BANKING EMPIRE

The Butcher family was arguably the most influential family in Maynardville, Tennessee. Its patriarch, Cecil Butcher, owned and operated the only bank in Union County as well as a popular grocery store. Just about everyone in the area knew and respected the affable Butcher.

Everyone in the county expected Cecil's sons, Jake and C.H., to follow in their father's footsteps. However, after Jake married movie star Sonya Wilde and C.H. married his high school sweetheart, Shirley Rutherford, the brothers became partners as they started several disparate companies. These ventures were all successful, and in 1968, with financial assistance from their father, the brothers were able to purchase the First National Bank of Lake City, Tennessee. It was the first of many banks the brothers would acquire in the next several years.

On August 23, 1968, the Butcher brothers and Harry D. Vestal took control of the bank in Lake City, and Vestal became its president. Just one month after the Butchers gained control of this small bank, federal regulators from their Memphis office warned them about questionable banking practices. The warnings included the regulators' concerns about making internal loans and paying extraordinarily large salaries to part-time employees.

In 1969, Jake and C.H. formed the City and County Banking Group. They were now in control of twenty-seven banks in Tennessee and Kentucky. The brothers' success was without precedent in the history of banking in the United States. Jake felt that he was now ready to start planning the mansion he had promised Sonya when they got married.

Cecil Butcher's original bank. *Author's collection.*

Butcher's Red Gate Horse Farm. *Author's collection.*

In 1970, C.H. and Shirley Butcher moved into an eighteen-room house on Black Oak Ridge, just north of Knoxville. Its furnishings included oriental rugs and priceless antiques. The master bedroom measured thirty-two by twenty-one feet and had a beamed cathedral ceiling, a stone fireplace and a Jacuzzi.

It was 1972 when construction began on Jake and Sonya's forty-room mansion, Whirlwind. The name for the mansion was derived from the fact that every time the doors were opened, the howling wind came through the spacious lobby.

The Butchers spared no expense in decorating the twenty-five-thousand-square-foot structure. Twelve heat pumps were required for the massive building. A full-time electrician was hired as well as a staff of eleven. Forty-seven telephone lines ran into the mansion.

Jake Butcher was now ready for the big time. He decided to run for governor of Tennessee in 1974. Newspaper advertisements read, "Jake Butcher will be a governor whose judgment you can trust."

When the polls closed on the Democrat primary election, Jake was beaten by Ray Blanton, who went on to win the general election and become the next Tennessee governor. Jake later took some solace in the fact that he had prophetically told friends that Blanton could be bought. Indeed, Blanton was eventually removed from office before his term expired after he was accused of issuing pardons to criminals in exchange for money. His replacement, Lamar Alexander, was sworn in three days early to prevent Blanton from issuing further pardons.

Jake ran for governor again in 1978. During that campaign, attorney G.W. Ridenour took control of Jake's banking interests. This time, Jake did not run as a country boy but as an experienced, successful banker. This time, however, he lost to incumbent Lamar Alexander by a count of 703,000 to 523,000.

Jake and Sonya Butcher's mansion, Whirlwind. Knoxville News-Sentinel.

Jake bought the anemic Hamilton National Bank in 1975 and changed its name to United American Bank. In 1977, Knoxville's United American Bank's ratio of total capital to total assets averaged 6.58 percent, which was below the minimum 7 percent ratio required by federal regulations.

Jake became tired of the constant demands by the regulators and pulled United American out of the Federal Reserve System. The chairman of the Federal Deposit Insurance Corporation would later say, "United American operated on the fringe of soundness. It eschewed caution in favor of leverage, reasonable conservatism in favor of aggressiveness and diversification in favor of real estate concentration and loans to insiders and quasi-insiders and their interests."

Construction began in 1976 on Jake's twenty-seven-story United American Bank building in downtown Knoxville. A helicopter landing pad was constructed on the top of the building so that Jake could commute between his office and Whirlwind. The sixth floor was the nerve center of the Butcher banking empire. Jake's office was in the southeast corner of the floor. C.H. occupied the northeast corner.

Club LeConte, sitting atop the United American building, offered a panoramic view that included the Smoky Mountains. It was furnished with plush furniture and deep-pile carpet. It became the hangout for the Butchers, business associates and political friends. Exotic food and vintage wines were always on hand.

Bank regulators who oversaw the $3 billion in Butcher banks were often lavishly entertained at Club LeConte, greatly alarming top management at the FDIC. To several managers of that organization, which was formed because of the large number of bank losses during the Great Depression, red flags were flying. Even though rumors of rampant banking irregularities at the Butcher banks were being discussed in Tennessee and in Washington, D.C., this news presumably never got to FDIC's president, William Isaac.

Only a small number of people knew that the Butcher brothers were receiving tips as to when to expect a "surprise" inspection by bank inspectors. Jesse Barr, an acquaintance of the Butchers, whom they appointed to a high-ranking executive position, received this type of notice for years. In her book *Whirlwind*, Sandra Lea wrote the following:

> A week's warning meant a lot to a "red flag" bank. A lot could happen in one week with a man like Jesse Barr in place to transfer bad loans to other banks. Jesse would spend hours on the phone transferring questionable loans totaling tens of millions of dollars into banks not under immediate scrutiny.

Jake Butcher's bank building (left) and C.H. Butcher's bank building (right) in downtown Knoxville. *Author's collection.*

Hundreds of millions of dollars in sour loans were effectively hidden this way from bank examiners for many years. During bank examinations, examiners would go to Jesse's 23rd story office to question the non-banker concerning particular problems they needed help with. Jesse was always pleased to accommodate them.

For most observers, the rapid success that Jake and C.H. were enjoying was amazing. Their success prompted state Speaker of the House Ned McWherter to say: "Jake Butcher's going to keep on so that he won't want to run for governor next time. He'll own the entire state. He'll own the capitol building. We'll have a drive-in window on the left side of the thing."

Jake reportedly said: "I've never been given anything but a good name and a good family. I never inherited any money or stole any, so the only way I can get it is to borrow it. We'd borrow money, buy a bank, *pay it off*, and then borrow money to buy another."

In reality, bank loans hardly ever got paid off. Shill companies were set up so that money could be loaned to them, with the proceeds going to support the tremendous loans that were growing more unmanageable every day. Fake loans were entered into their books to people who knew nothing of the loans they were supposed to have executed.

Years later, Jesse Barr described the pressure-cooker environment in which he was working as Jake Butcher's right-hand man:

Every day was a new world for me. Office hours were a constant series of crises. Jake's spending was out of control. He had mortgaged himself to the hilt to buy up his banks. He was still burdened by his campaign debts. Back in 1981, before he bought the bank in Lexington, his monthly living expenses and his monthly interest payments were about $500,000. When he bought the two other banks, his debt went up to $20 million, and his interest and living costs went to $2 million a month. He once bought a $600,000 yacht and didn't tell me about it.

The first thing Barr did every morning was raise cash necessary to keep the system afloat. He generally did this by selling loans to other banks in the Butcher network. He usually promised to buy the loans back if they became too hot to handle.

Then for Barr, overdrafts started coming in.

One day we might have $500,000 in Nashville or $800,000 in Knoxville. The Butchers' constant drain on their banks would show up first in one account, then in another. So, I would worry about them for the next hour. I'd work on the World's Fair [a project Jake was involved in] a little bit, work on the private companies awhile, then go to a luncheon up at the Club LeConte where we had a private dining room. We had lunches up there just about every day.

Huge financial decisions were often made at these luncheons.

The next day, Barr would start implementing Jake's decisions, which often added to his stack of problems. Sometimes, Jake knew nothing of the problems. Barr said: "Jake was PR man, a front man. He didn't want to hear about a lot of problems."

In 1980, the Butcher brothers divided their empire into two entities. In several quarters, this raised suspicions that this might make it easier for them to conduct illegal banking activities. William Isaac, chairman of the FDIC, said: "I view this as one bank with a lot of branches. That's not legally what it is, but that as a matter of fact was the way it was operated." Investigative reporters from *The Tennessean* found that the loans within the Butcher banks were "as intertwined as spaghetti in a can."

As early as 1976, Knoxville mayor Kyle Testerman appointed a committee to look into the feasibility of the city's hosting a World's Fair. Jake was appointed chairman of the committee.

The nation first heard about Knoxville's planned World's Fair when it was prominently mentioned on the lead float in President Ronald Reagan's inaugural parade in January 1981. The previous year, Congress had appropriated $20.8 million for participation of the United States in the Fair, and Great Britain, France, Germany and China agreed to sponsor exhibits. Butcher banks, United American and the City and County Bank of Knox County financed approximately $50 million of World's Fair loans.

The Fair's theme structure was the Sunsphere, which was designed by architect William Denton, who had designed Jake's mansion, Whirlwind. The golden globe rises 266 feet in the air and sits on a 192-foot-high tower. The globe symbolizes the sun to represent the World's Fair theme, "Energy."

Knoxville's World's Fair opened on May 1, 1982, to a crowd of eighty-seven-thousand people, including President Reagan, who was there to officially open the Fair. The opening had fireworks, a twenty-one-gun salute, fourteen high school bands and sixty thousand balloons. Everyone present agreed that it was a day to be remembered. Everything at the Fair was rosy, but a dark cloud was forming over the vast Butcher banking empire.

In April, a month before the World's Fair opened, bank regulators requested a meeting with Jake and the United American board of directors. Jake asked for the meeting to be delayed because everyone was preoccupied. Ironically, the meeting was finally held in May, just as the Fair was opening. At that meeting, the regional director of the FDIC told the United American directors, "Your bank is in serious trouble and must resolve its problems by the end of the year." The bank's reserve had reached a point where the regulators were concerned that if many bad loans materialized, the losses could not be covered.

The opulent lifestyle of the Butcher families is characterized by the way they celebrated Christmas in 1981. Sonya said that there were 250 presents wrapped at her house for family, friends and associates. If she ran short on presents, she would "go to the silver cabinet and pull something out and wrap it."

Jake's seven-year-old son, Jason, received a 1970 Dodge automobile similar to the one in the television show *The Dukes of Hazzard*. Sonya received a Russian sable coat valued at $30,000.

At Butch-Vue, C.H. and Shirley's home, Shirley received a Rolls-Royce valued at $165,000. She drove it around with the price sticker on the car

Right: Sunsphere from the 1982 World's Fair. *Author's collection.*

Below: Amphitheater from the Knoxville World's Fair. *Author's collection.*

Left: President Jimmy Carter visits Jake Butcher and Senator James Sasser. Knoxville News-Sentinel.

Below, from left to right: Honey Alexander, Lamar Alexander, President Ronald Reagan, and Jake Butcher. Knoxville News-Sentinel.

window for several months.

The following transactions are an insight into the Butcher banking empire at that time. Natural Energy Mining Inc., a Butcher company, borrowed $1.75 million on October 16, 1981, from C&C Bank of Anderson County. Jake's bookkeeper, Judy Franklin, had signed the note and was listed as secretary of Natural Energy Mining. The proceeds of the loan were deposited in the account of JFB Petroleum and Land Company, which then diverted a large portion to Jake to pay off his debts. In 1982, Natural Energy Mining borrowed another $675,000 from C&C Bank. The proceeds were routed through United American Bank into Jake's personal account. Later in 1982, Natural Energy Mining borrowed $1.75 million from C&C Bank. Jake-controlled entities received $756,000 from this transaction.

As had been the case for years, the fact that Jake would be receiving a major portion of the loan proceeds was not revealed to the lending institutions. This allowed him to conceal from bank examiners that he was receiving payment from loans that greatly exceeded a particular bank's lending limit.

In 1981 and 1982, Natural Energy Mining Company received over $10 million in loans. Jake's assistants falsified the books that pertained to the businesses and banks involved in these transactions. Jake was now funneling large amounts of money from his banks through Natural Energy Mining into his personal accounts. Many more similar operations were underway at this time.

Knoxville's World's Fair closed on October 31, 1982. More than 86,000 visitors, wearing "I Was There" buttons, were somewhat melancholy as they watched the Fair's final fireworks flicker out over the Tennessee River. Over its six-month life, Fair visitors totaled 11,127,786.

In describing the World's Fair's success, its chairman, Jake Butcher, said: "We were financially successful. It brings out the pride in us mountain folk and proves that a town of less than 200,000 could do what most people thought we couldn't, have a successful World's Fair."

None of the visitors were aware that on October 25, 1982, six days prior to the closing of the World's Fair, federal and state regulators began examining Butcher banks in Kentucky.

Jake and C.H. celebrated late into the night after the World's Fair closed, and both slept in the next day, November 1, 1982. Top assistant Jesse Barr was in his office early that morning when he got a call from a bank employee telling him that several examiners had shown up at the United American Bank. He fixed a Bloody Mary and called and woke up Jake. Soon afterward, he got calls from employees at C&C Bank telling him that examiners were there as well. After he called and woke up C.H., Barr sat there wondering what was going on. The Butchers had always been warned when examiners were coming.

Approximately 180 bank examiners in Tennessee and Kentucky converged on every bank in the Butcher empire. One bank official said: "When the auditors came in, it was almost like a death knell. After we found out they were not just in United American but in all the banks, it was like doom."

Early in 1983, the Butcher banking empire was collapsing. Managers at over two dozen of their banks discovered that the United American stock they held as collateral for the loans they held was worthless. In January, the Regional Director of the FDIC addressed a gathering of the United American board members. The members sat in stunned silence as they were told, "Your bank is insolvent." Chief bank examiner, Ronny Parham, told them that the entire situation surrounding the Butcher banks was "almost beyond comprehension. I'm not used to seeing this much wrong. More than $90 million in loans should be written off as losses or considered of doubtful nature."

More ominous, ten days prior to the shutdown of the banks, the FDIC requested a criminal investigation into the irregularities at the Butcher banks. The examiners were uncovering large numbers of forged loan documents, securities violations, and the shredding of bank records.

In March 1983, federal bank examiners put C.H.'s banks under a "cease and desist" order, whereby loans could no longer be shifted from one bank to another. This did not stop friends and family members from withdrawing large sums of money, which began after the collapse of Jake's United American Bank. Jake's sister-in-law Anne Wilde withdrew $378,000; Wilma Browder, the mother of Anne Wilde, withdrew $236,500; Ed Browder, father of Anne Wilde and a United American Bank director, withdrew $225,000; Marshall Rutherford, C.H. Butcher's nephew, withdrew $111,500; C.H.'s brother-in-law Carley Rutherford withdrew $57,819; Innis Steiner, a relative to the president of one of C.H.'s banks, withdrew $101,000; and E.J. Steiner, the bank president's father, withdrew $50,427.

On the day of the "Saint Valentine's Day Massacre," Jake was refused entry by federal agents into his own United American Bank in Knoxville. When he saw what was happening, he mumbled, "You gotta be kiddin."

A few months later, when asked by reporters if the bad press he was receiving bothered him, he replied:

You know, I really worry about it. I'm embarrassed. It's been horrible. I read recently from a national publication that I was lying around the pool, had plenty of time and a dark tan. I get up in the mornings so nervous I want to throw up. People really need to know the truth about just how devastating it has been. Except for being sick yourself or having your children sick, the next worse thing is public disgrace....

A lot of people run into me and say, "You know Jake, you look pretty good." It's like they expected me to have aged 30 years and just be shriveled up and barely hanging onto life. Maybe inside I am. I don't know. On the outside I am trying to keep my composure and my health....You try to analyze what went wrong, and then you feel embarrassed about it and you feel hurt. Then you try to pull yourself together. You say, well, my life is not going to end that way, I am not going to become an alcoholic. I am not going to shoot myself. I am going to stay together one way or the other and take care of my responsibilities as a father and a husband.

In September 1983, Sonya Butcher declared in a sworn affidavit that her name had been forged on a loan to one of her husband's companies. She claimed that her signature was one of twenty-six forgeries at banks controlled by the Butchers. By that time, the FBI had discovered forged documents on fifteen other loans.

A rush of people came forward claiming they had not borrowed money from Butcher banks. Paul Wiley told investigators that a $469,651 note in his name was a forgery. Hugh Rule said he never borrowed $286,000 that was in the Butchers' books. Milton Turner denied borrowing a similar $286,000 amount. Robert Windham said he never borrowed the $100,000 as recorded. Michael Downing denied borrowing $80,974.

On November 15, 1983, a congressional committee disclosed that the FDIC had turned over to the Department of Justice forty-eight cases of suspected criminal wrongdoing in Butcher banks. A seventy-three-page report by the congressional committee concluded that the failure of the Butcher banks was the largest in the history of the United States. The $219 million that had to be paid by the FDIC insurance fund was three times that of the three previous bank failures combined.

Writer Sandra Lea described the situation in which the Butcher families found themselves in 1984:

> *Now they were deserted, stranded like beached whales on a barren island. They had become a burden too heavy to lift, too tainted with shame, and their solitude was a torment not threatened even in hell....They were stripped naked now for all of the world to see, that very world which was once at their feet. And the house of Butcher was exposed as a fragile house of cards, all deuces, built on a foundation of fraud and deception....Their main activity now revolved around trips to the courthouse....Hope was beginning to dwindle now to a frantic desire to merely keep their heads out of the executioner's noose, as many who were caught in the Butcher's destructive wake demanded their blood as the only propitiation for the loss of their gold.*

On November 14, 1984, Jake was indicted in Knoxville on forty-four federal charges of bank fraud. He voluntarily turned himself in to FBI agents and was taken to the Knox County courthouse in handcuffs. The combined charges he faced amounted to a maximum of 220 years in prison. The indictments were sixty-four pages long.

One week later, Jake was charged in a thirty-two-page indictment in Memphis. The charges included bank robbery, mail fraud, wire fraud, misapplication of funds, conspiracy, falsification of bank records and false statements on a loan application. The combined charges in the Memphis indictments amounted to a maximum of 170 years in prison. Things got even worse for Jake when, in March 1985, he was charged with federal income tax evasion.

With Jake facing so many years of possible jail time, on April 22, 1985, Federal Judge William Thomas announced to a packed courtroom that Jake and the federal government had agreed to a deal. Jake would agree to plead guilty to twenty charges that included defrauding his banks out of $17 million and to filing false income taxes for two years. The maximum prison time would be twenty years; the minimum prison time would be six years and nine months.

When sentencing Jake, Judge Thomas made the following statement:

> *The investigation by federal authorities clearly disclosed that you undertook to steal millions and millions of dollars from the depositors of the banks which you controlled. Your multi-million-dollar fraud was, if not the sole cause, at least a contributing cause of United American Bank's failure.... Your offenses are of the highest severity.*
>
> *Your use of multiple frauds to illegally obtain millions from your own banks warrants a sentence comparable to one that would be imposed on a person who uses violence, or the threat of violence, to obtain a far smaller amount of money from one of your own banks.*

Jake stood and said in a soft voice: "I want to apologize for what I have done. I hope the Knoxville community will give me a chance to repay any debt, anything I've hurt anyone for. I never intended anything wrong for anyone." Judge Thomas then sentenced him to six years and eight months in a federal prison. After serving six years in prison, Jake was released in November 1991.

In January 1986, C.H. Butcher was arrested by FBI agents. He was charged with eleven counts of mail fraud, ten counts of wire fraud and five counts of securities fraud. In a six-week-long trial, C.H. was found not guilty. Forty-eight hours later, he was charged with federal tax violations that went back several years. The forty-one-count indictment was for allegedly filing fraudulent tax deductions.

C.H. had been in bankruptcy for several months in 1986 when he was hit with charges by federal agents for bankruptcy fraud. He and Shirley were indicted for concealing millions of dollars' worth of assets from their creditors after they were forced into bankruptcy. C.H., facing a maximum time in prison of 285 years, in January 1987, agreed to a 25-year plea deal with federal prosecutors. After serving seven years in prison, C.H. was released in February 1993.

As free men, the brothers lived largely subsistence lives the rest of their days. They were unable to pay back any of the millions in debt they owed in perpetuity. C.H. died at sixty-two in 2002. Jake died at eighty-one in 2017.

13

"I NEVER INTENDED TO BECOME A KILLER"

The community of Heiskell, Tennessee, is located on the northern edge of Knox County. Ridges there are prominent features in the Ridge and Valley Province that lies between the Great Smoky Mountains and the Cumberland Mountains. Level and fertile bottomland is scarce and therefore prized. Most farming can be described as truck farming, and most of the locals have other jobs to supplement any income they receive from farming.

Clarence Leon Raby lived in this small community. He had little education and few skills to speak of, so he depended heavily on work he could pick up from neighboring farmers. His neighbors agreed that he was a good worker, and they were always glad to hire him when they needed help in their tobacco patches and hay fields, or when they were building fences.

Shock, dismay and disbelief gripped Raby's neighbors when word spread that he was the subject of a massive manhunt. They wondered, "What happened that would cause the neighborhood boy to be in so much trouble?" Then, to a person, they started locking their doors and loading their weapons.

The neighbors would soon learn that a crime spree had its beginning when Raby was stopped by a Knox County deputy sheriff for driving erratically. He was arrested for drunk driving. A few days later, Raby was convicted and sent to the Knox County Workhouse, just east of Knoxville.

While in the Workhouse, Raby became acquainted with another inmate named Billy McCoy who was serving time for forgery. The two carefully laid out a plan and executed it perfectly to escape from the fenced-in and heavily guarded facility. The date was July 6, 1960. Unbelievably, each had only about three weeks left to serve on their respective sentences.

The escapees managed to elude the police during the night, and the next morning, July 7, they were able to steal an automobile from the driveway of a home on Cement Road in East Knox County, not far from the Workhouse.

Like much of his life, Raby once again found himself short of cash and, along with his newly found accomplice, was in dire straits. Knowing the area well, Raby suggested that he knew where they could easily get some badly needed money.

Andersonville, Tennessee, is only about ten miles from the community where Raby was raised, and he had been there several times. He knew the location of a service station that was owned and operated by an old man who would almost certainly be easy to rob. The two drove there in their stolen Pontiac.

Going to the service station was perhaps their biggest mistake. When told he was being robbed and that he was to hand over his money, the station's owner, Frank Keith, pulled his gun in an effort to fight them off. He was promptly shot in the chest with a shotgun before he could pull the trigger of his own weapon. When Raby and McCoy went into the station, they were escapees, but in a few minutes, as their victim lay on the floor mortally wounded, they became murderers.

As the two escapees were running from the service station with a bag of cash, a man and his wife arrived at the station to purchase gas. The woman decided to go inside the service station. Just as she was entering through the station door, she was startled by two men who rushed by her. The lady was so curious that she went to the rear of the station office to see if she could determine what was going on. She found a dying Frank Keith lying on the floor. He told the lady: "You can't help me. It's too late." When deputies arrived at the scene, they realized that they would be searching for armed fugitives.

The two customers at the service station told police they saw two men jump in a Pontiac and speed away. Later in the day, deputies found the burned hulk of the stolen car near the Anderson and Knox County line.

Anderson County Sheriff Glad Woodward had warrants sworn out that charged Clarence Leon Raby and Billy McCoy with robbery and murder. The Federal Bureau of Investigation issued federal fugitive warrants against both of them and added them to its Ten Most Wanted list.

Federal agents were able to locate and arrest McCoy six weeks later in Chicago. He told the investigators that at first he and Raby had fled to

Left: Clarence Leon Raby. Knoxville News-Sentinel.

Below: FBI flyer pertaining to Clarence Raby. Knoxville News-Sentinel.

IDENTIFICATION
ORDER NO. 3390
August 4, 1960

W⊕nted by ⟨FBI⟩

FBI No.
5,097,878

INTERSTATE FLIGHT – MURDER
CLARENCE LEON RABY

ALIASES: LEON BATES, CLARANCE RABY, CLARENCE RABY, CLEARENCE RABY,
CLEARENCE LEON RABY, CLEARNCE RABY

20 M 1 T-t 19
L 3 W

Photographs taken 1958

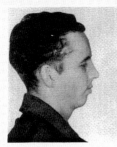

Clarence Leon Raby

DESCRIPTION
AGE: 27, born September 2, 1932, Claiborne County, Tennessee
HEIGHT: 6'
COMPLEXION: ruddy
WEIGHT: 150 to 155 pounds
RACE: white
BUILD: slender
NATIONALITY: American
HAIR: brown, wavy
OCCUPATIONS: electrician,
EYES: blue
mechanic, service station
attendant, welder
SCARS AND MARKS: 2" scar right cheek crossing over jawbone, 1" scar
between ring finger and little finger, right hand; tattoos, 6" dagger
and snake left forearm, flowers on right forearm, scroll upper right
arm, sailing ship on chest.

CRIMINAL RECORD
Raby has been convicted of purse snatching, interstate transportation
of a stolen motor vehicle, petty larceny and burglary.

CAUTION
RABY IS WANTED FOR A BRUTAL SHOTGUN MURDER COMMITTED DURING A ROBBERY
AND IS ALSO BEING SOUGHT FOR THE COLD-BLOODED MURDER OF A DEPUTY
SHERIFF. HE IS BELIEVED TO BE ARMED WITH SHOTGUNS AND REVOLVERS,
INCLUDING A .357 MAGNUM. RABY MAY BE ACCOMPANIED BY BILLY MC COY, FBI
IDENTIFICATION ORDER NO. 3391. BOTH SHOULD BE CONSIDERED EXTREMELY
DANGEROUS.

A Federal warrant was issued at Knoxville, Tennessee, on July 11, 1960, charging Raby with unlawful interstate flight to avoid prosecution for murder (Title 18, U. S. Code, Section 1073).

IF YOU HAVE INFORMATION CONCERNING THIS PERSON, PLEASE NOTIFY ME OR CONTACT YOUR
LOCAL FBI OFFICE. PHONE NUMBER IS LISTED BELOW. OTHER OFFICES ARE LISTED ON BACK.

IDENTIFICATION
ORDER NO. 3390

DIRECTOR
Federal Bureau of Investigation
Washington 25, D. C.

MURDER & MAYHEM IN EAST TENNESSEE

North Carolina. A few days later, they decided it might be better if they went different ways. McCoy made his way to Chicago, but the police thought it was likely that Raby would not stay away very long from the ridges and valleys he knew so well. In the meantime, McCoy was extradited to the Anderson County jail. He identified Raby as the one who had pulled the trigger of the gun that killed Frank Keith.

One month after the killing of Frank Keith, authorities were still convinced that Raby was hiding in the general area comprising parts of Anderson, Knox and Union Counties. In addition to the continuous ridges and valleys, there were several limestone caves in which a fugitive could easily hide.

Local lawmen and federal agents along with their bloodhounds began a campaign to meticulously search this area. The lawmen and their dogs were often seen resting at local grocery stores and drinking cold drinks completely covered with mud from crawling through the caves in the area. It became so commonplace that locals knew what they had been doing without asking. Seeing the muddied posse so often was unsettling for the area's residents. In addition to having all doors and windows locked, residents now kept multiple weapons loaded and ready.

Just about every day, the police received reports of Raby sightings. Every time a sighting was reported, the police would set up roadblocks at every intersection in the area. Some sightings were genuine; some were not. For instance, dozens of policemen quickly converged on a large culvert under the road when they received a "hot" tip that Raby had been seen entering the culvert. It was likely that he had been there a short time earlier, but the officers once again found nothing. It seemed that the police, who were by now becoming demoralized, were always late getting to a reported sighting.

One day, Raby was spotted in North Knoxville, and a footrace between Raby and the police ensued. Almost totally exhausted, he sat down in someone's comfortable outdoor rocking chair and more or less waited to be captured. To his surprise, the chasing policemen who saw him relaxing in the rocker went charging right on by. When they were out of sight, he slipped back into the woods and was gone again.

It seemed that Clarence Raby had much of East Tennessee bobbing and weaving. This was partly because, as the police believed at the time and a belief that was later substantiated, the young man was getting assistance from some of the locals. A few people reported that on some nights their gardens were raided. There were unproven rumors that Raby was actually back in the fields working for some of his former employers while the massive manhunt was underway.

Drainage pipe where lawmen thought they had Raby trapped. *Author's collection.*

During the weeks of the manhunt, Raby's family members welcomed all newspaper and television reporters who called looking for a story. They indicated that they had no idea of his whereabouts and at the same time interjected that he had been "likable" until he discovered alcohol. Then, everything seemed to change. They told reporters that things really changed when drugs entered the picture. His sister said, "He was always a wild boy, but never downright mean."

On August 1, with police seemingly everywhere, Raby showed up at a house on Heiskell Road in northern Knox County. He held the two nervous residents at gunpoint for over an hour as he sat in their living room and tried to figure out his next move. The man and woman were fortunate, as Raby only took cash, guns and their Buick. From a personal standpoint, letting the couple live was not a good decision. Within five minutes, an all-points bulletin went out with the information that he was now in the couple's stolen Buick and likely on the road.

Fully aware that the couple would call the police, Raby quickly drove north to Union County and then west into Anderson County. He realized that he needed to abandon the Buick that every policeman was now looking for. Fred Rutherford was in his pickup truck in his driveway waiting to turn onto Hickory Valley Road when Raby stopped the stolen Buick and, at gunpoint, took Rutherford hostage. While Raby was in the process of stealing the truck and holding Rutherford at gunpoint, Union County Deputy Sheriff Ben Devault, who had pursued Raby into Anderson County, arrived on the scene and jumped out of his car with pistol drawn. Knowing the danger that the desperate Raby posed, the deputy quickly fired a single shot, which missed Raby. Almost simultaneously, Raby managed to fire two shots. Both of his shots struck the deputy, who died a few minutes later in the middle of the intersection of Hickory Valley Road and Bryam's Fork Road.

The double murderer then forced Rutherford to lie down in the bed of his own truck. The truck reached a speed of close to one hundred miles an hour as it raced west down Hinds Creek Road. The speed itself startled residents so much that they rushed into their houses and locked their doors. Some reported that they could see Rutherford's shirt flapping in the wind above the truck bed. With all of the publicity surrounding Raby and the

Intersection where Deputy DeVault was killed. *Jerry Kerr*.

Fred Rutherford's driveway, where he was kidnapped. *Jerry Kerr.*

ongoing local manhunt, the residents were almost certain that it was Raby driving a stolen vehicle and were sure that the man in the truck bed was another victim.

Rutherford, aware that he was in mortal danger, was completely surprised when Raby abruptly stopped the truck about one mile west of the Norris Freeway and Hinds Creek Road intersection and motioned for Rutherford to get out of the truck. Raby sped away, leaving behind a stunned Fred Rutherford. The way he treated Rutherford and the couple on Heiskell Road whose car he had stolen earlier in the day after holding them hostage seemed to indicate that Raby would kill only when someone was aiming a gun at him.

Shaken and realizing that Raby could return at any minute, Rutherford started walking in the fields instead of along the road. A suspicious resident reported him to the police. A policeman picked him up and, after hearing his hair-raising story, drove him home. All officers were promptly alerted to Raby's general location. The lawmen were now reasonably sure that they had the fugitive trapped. Ensuing events proved once again their thinking to be overly optimistic.

After crossing back into Knox County from Anderson County, Raby was spotted once again in the stolen truck. He was obviously going in broad circles and never straying far from his family's home. The police had been correct in their belief that he would remain in the area.

The killer had now returned to Knox County, the domain of Sheriff E.B. Bowles. Bowles owned a popular produce store and, during his election campaign, had passed out free bananas to prospective voters. He was elected even though he had no previous law enforcement experience. Elected in 1958, for two years Bowles and his administration had been dogged by alleged corruption and numerous scandals that included illegal use of taxpayer money, hiring deputies with criminal records and making wrongful arrests.

Sheriff Bowles was working on his reelection campaign and was not present in the fields and woods the day a sizable posse attempted to surround Raby. In his absence, Bowles had placed James Colquitt in charge. Colquitt had the nickname "Quick Draw McGraw," because he had accidentally shot an innocent bystander while making an arrest. On another occasion, he accidentally fired a shot inside a Knoxville television studio while demonstrating some new pistols the Sheriff's Department had recently acquired.

Suddenly, it sounded like a war had started when Colquitt and another deputy opened fire on two men in the fields ahead of them. These men had made the unfortunate decision to voluntarily join a posse that was helping with the Raby search. The two men who were hit were Kaley Cooper and his son Dan. Kaley survived, but Dan died from the gunshot wounds.

Immediately, the sheriff and his deputies started a public relations campaign that claimed the Coopers had opened fire on them first. They stated that the deputies had fired only in self-defense. The subsequent coroner's report and doctor's observations, however, indicated that both men had been shot in the back.

When a county employee corroborated the sheriff's tale, he was rewarded with a job as Deputy Sheriff. Unbelievably, the new deputy soon retracted his statement and, within a few weeks, killed himself.

Finally, during the night of August 28, 1960, a dog owned by Dillon Summers started barking loudly. With a loaded weapon, Summers went out on his front porch. Out of the darkness walked Clarence Raby, who calmly asked Summers to call Raby's parents. He indicated to Summers that he wanted to give himself up because he felt sure that he would be shot on sight in the process of trying to surrender. At that time, he said something to the effect of, "I know now how a fox feels when the hounds are closing in." It appeared that the desperate chase that had lasted for nearly two months was finally coming to an end.

Raby's brother Frank quickly came and picked Clarence up as he stood beside Heiskell Road just below Summers's house. He took his brother to the family home on Gamble Road, and as had been arranged by a telephone call from a member of Raby's family, Sheriff Bowles was there waiting for him.

Bowles lost the election, and just three days after the capture of Raby, a new sheriff was sworn in. Herman Wayland indicated that he was willing to surrender the killer to Anderson County authorities, but for the present, he thought it might be better to keep him in jail in Knox County for safekeeping. Once again, this would prove to be wishful thinking.

While in jail, Raby was interviewed several times. During one of these sessions, he was reported to have said, "I never intended to become a killer." He had been shocked and dismayed when Keith, the elderly service station owner, decided to defend himself.

A few days after Raby was placed in jail, his mother, sister and girlfriend came to visit. And, like a scene from an old Western movie, as investigators later concluded, the visitors brazenly smuggled in a weapon. Unfortunately, the saga was still not over.

During the night of October 24, 1960, Raby asked to make another statement. As was the custom, he was removed from his cell and taken to an interrogation room. At the end of this session, he was led back to his cell. When he, Tennessee Bureau of Investigation agent Walter Bearden and a Tennessee Highway patrol sergeant entered the cell, Raby quickly pulled a .357 Magnum pistol from above the cell door.

One of the startled policemen said, "Where did you get that thing?" Bearden later reported that the inmate was holding the weapon with both hands and appeared to be very nervous as he kept cocking and uncocking the gun. He said, "I did not know if it would go off or not."

A desperate Raby held the weapon on both lawmen and a jailer and instructed them to lead him out of the cellblock and down the elevator. He said loudly: "I ain't going to no damn electric chair for killing anybody. I mean business. I'm going out!"

Blind bad luck struck Raby when the elevator door opened at the first floor. It just happened to be during the 10:00 p.m. shift change, and he immediately saw that the hallway was crowded with armed deputies. Grasping the ominous situation, a panicked Raby went running down the hall wildly shooting in every direction. He emptied his gun but managed to snatch the desk sergeant's pistol as he rushed by.

Coincidentally, Deputy Kenny Milligan was entering the hallway with a man he had just arrested for drunk driving. Raby, now with the deputy's fully loaded pistol, was again firing in every direction. Deputy Milligan heard the gunshots and running feet and immediately realized a jailbreak was underway. He later told the *Knoxville News-Sentinel*: "Two bullets hit me [one came within less than an inch of his heart] knocking me to the floor. I don't know if he jumped over me or not. I kinda raised up on my elbow and fired five times at the running man. I saw him stagger, then kinda fall out the front door."

Clarence Leon Raby, with three bullets lodged in his stomach, stumbled down the outside steps of the jail and came to rest faceup. A curious crowd gathered as Raby's tragic life came to an end. He was twenty-eight years old. The spree that was started by a man who said he had never intended to be a murderer was over at long last.

Raby's family had difficulty finding a church that would offer its facilities for a funeral. Mount Harmony Baptist Church, which is located about one mile from the Raby home, allowed the funeral to be held there. Clarence Leon Raby was laid to rest in the church's cemetery.

Mount Harmony Baptist Church, the site of Clarence Raby's funeral. *Author's collection.*

Clarence Leon Raby's tombstone.
Author's collection.

Deputy Milligan received numerous congratulatory letters from across the United States but showed little interest in them. He did not even open several of them. He said: "I don't believe in shooting people. I'd rather forget about it and go back to work." When Milligan had sufficiently recovered from his serious wounds and was released from the hospital, he went directly to Raby's family and apologized.

Raby's mother, sister and girlfriend were tried for slipping a weapon to Raby in jail and were found to be not guilty. Billy McCoy, Raby's accomplice, was not as fortunate. His trial netted him twenty-one years in prison for his part in the killing of Frank Keith at Keith's service station—the event that started it all.

EPILOGUE

Don Severance, the high-school student who took Fred Hankins to Hensley Motor Service and then drove him home, a few years later flew fighter jets for the United States Air Force in Vietnam.

Brushy Mountain State Penitentiary ceased being a prison in 2009 and is now a popular museum.

Jim Hackworth currently owns the estate that was previously owned by Dr. Hyram and Yvonne Kitchen and has continued raising horses there.

The surviving descendants of the Richards siblings, Mary and Joseph, kept possession of the Oliver Springs mansion until 1941, when they sold it to the American Legion for one dollar. The building burned in 1947.

Ann Street in Oliver Springs is named for the grandmother of the murdered Richards sisters, one of whom was also named Ann.

The box of letters that Fern Drinnen had packed in 1944 was discovered in 2010. Through these letters, the three Drinnen sons, who had been very young when their father died, got an insight into his personality and could see the obvious concern and love he had for them. Fern died in 1995 at eighty-seven.

In October 1977, National Park Ranger Jack Collier purchased at auction the station wagon that the alleged mass murderer William Bradford Bishop Jr. used to transport his deceased family. Collier paid $1,750 for the vehicle.

In 1992, the federal government ended its policy of allowing the cabins in the Elkmont section of the Great Smoky Mountains National Park to be leased to private companies. The government assumed ownership of the cabins.

In 2004, twenty-eight years after the murder of the Bishop family, the FBI placed William Bishop on its Ten Most Wanted list in hopes that modern social media might help find him. No trace of him has ever been found.

Jake and Sonya Butcher's mansion, Whirlwind, still stands but is slowly deteriorating. The cost of restoring it far outweighs the value of the property if it was restored.

The Butcher brothers' bank buildings still stand as the tallest structures in downtown Knoxville.

BIBLIOGRAPHY

Allen, R.S., and Steve O. Watson. *The Perry's Camp Murders*. West Conshohocken, PA: Infinity Publishing, 2009.

Ashley, Danita. *Murder by the Springs*. Oliver Springs, TN: self-published, 2014.

Ayers, Hack. *Hills, Deals, and Stills*. Grand Rapids, MI: Credo House, 2015.

Baldwin, Juanitta. *Unsolved Disappearances in the Great Smoky Mountains*. Virginia Beach, VA: Suntop Press, 1998.

Brill, David. *Into the Mist*. Gatlinburg, TN: Great Smoky Mountain Association, 2017.

Ehle, John. *Trail of Tears*. Toronto: Anchor Books, 1998.

Gabbard, Alex. *Return to Thunder Road*. Lenoir City, TN: Gabbard Publications, 1992.

Knoxville News-Sentinel. "I'm Going Out." July 29, 2012.

———. "Lost Along the Highway." October 28, 2018.

Lea, Sandra. *Whirlwind*. Oak Ridge, TN: Self-published, 2000.

Los Angeles Times. "James Earl Ray, Wife Are Granted Divorce." March 5, 1993.

———. "Police Caution Veterinary College Deans." February 25, 1990.

McCarter, Dwight, and Ronald Schmidt. *Lost!* Yellow Springs, OH: Graphicom Press, 1998.

People Magazine. "Why Did a Nice Girl Like Anna Sandhu Wed James Earl Ray?" October 30, 1978.

Sides, Hampton. *Hellhound on His Trail*. New York: Anchor Books, 2011.

Treadway, David. "Biting Back: Animal Researchers, Industries Go on the Offensive Against Increasingly Militant Activists." *Los Angeles Times*, April 12, 1990.

Walker, Cas. *The White Caps of Sevier County.* Knoxville, TN: Trent Printing Company, 1937.

ABOUT THE AUTHOR

 ewaine Speaks graduated from the University of Tennessee with a major in economics. He retired in 2002 following a career in the marketing of industrial controls, both domestically and internationally. While at Knoxville Central High School, he was named All–East Tennessee in football and All-County in baseball. He went on to play outfield for the University of Tennessee Volunteers. While a member of the Tennessee Air National Guard in 1961, Speaks was sent to eastern France when President John Kennedy called several thousand guardsmen and reservists to active duty. For this deployment, he was awarded the Berlin Crisis medal. He was a member of the East Tennessee Veteran's Honor Guard for seventeen years and, during this time, received the Presidential Volunteer Service Award.

Also by Dewaine Speaks:
East Tennessee in World War II
Historic Disasters of East Tennessee
Preparing for International Travel
Weston Fulton Changed the World

Visit us at
www.historypress.com
....